Aerial Surveys of Cliff-Nesting Raptors

in the National Petroleum Reserve–Alaska, 1999, with Comparisons to 1977

Technical Note 413

By

Robert J. Ritchie,
Ann M. Wildman, and
David A. Yokel

U.S. DEPARTMENT OF THE INTERIOR
Bureau of Land Management
1150 University Avenue
Fairbanks, Alaska 99709

December 2003

Suggested citation:

Ritchie, Robert J., Ann M. Wildman, and David A. Yokel. 2003. Aerial surveys of cliff-nesting raptors in the National Petroleum Reserve–Alaska, 1999, with comparisons to 1977. Technical Note 413. Bureau of Land Management, Denver, Colorado. BLM/AK/ST-03/016+6501+023. 66 pp.

Contents

List of Figures

List of Tables

List of Tables (continued)

Abstract

In summer 1999, an extensive aerial survey of cliff-nesting raptors was conducted in the National Petroleum Reserve–Alaska (NPR–A) on Alaska's North Slope. No similarly extensive survey had been conducted since 1977. In the interim, the regional population of the Arctic peregrine falcon (*Falco peregrinus tundrius*) had increased, as shown by monitoring along the Colville River. The 1999 survey assessed the present abundance and distribution of the peregrine falcon, as well as the gyrfalcon (*Falco rusticolus*), golden eagle (*Aquila chrysaetos*), and rough-legged hawk (*Buteo lagopus*) in most of the NPR–A. Specifically excluded from the 1999 survey were the Kogosukruk and Kikiakrorak Rivers and the Colville River below its junction with the Etivluk River. These areas had been included in other recent surveys. Peregrine falcons were found occupying 67 sites in 1999, 61 of which were in the area surveyed in 1977 and in which only four occupied sites were found. Gyrfalcons nest earlier than other raptor species in the NPR–A, and the 1999 survey was conducted too late in the season to determine occupancy of many sites. Gyrfalcons were located at only 19 sites in 1999, down from 29 in 1977, but 41 sites showing evidence of gyrfalcon use were identified, whereas only 29 such sites were identified in 1977. Eleven pairs of golden eagles were found in 1999, which is similar to the 10 pairs found in 1977. Rough-legged hawks were the most abundant and widespread cliff-nesting raptors in the NPR–A in both years. Their relative distribution was similar in the 2 years, but twice as many pairs were found in 1999 (109) as in 1977 (55). The difficulties of comparing the results of the two surveys are discussed.

Photo by Ted Swem, U.S. Fish and Wildlife Service.

Introduction

In 1977, Ritchie (1979) conducted the first extensive aerial surveys specifically directed at locating and taking inventory of cliff-nesting raptors and evaluating habitats for these species in the National Petroleum Reserve–Alaska (NPR–A). The primary objectives of those surveys were to locate peregrine falcons (*Falco peregrinus tundrius*) outside the main Colville River corridor and evaluate habitat in the foothill and mountain provinces of the NPR–A for peregrine falcons, gyrfalcons (*Falco rusticolus*), golden eagles (*Aquila chrysaetos*), and rough-legged hawks (*Buteo lagopus*). Other raptor surveys in the area (Pegau 1975; Cade and White 1976) had been more limited in regional or species coverage.

The Bureau of Land Management (BLM), during evaluations of the potential effects of oil leasing, exploration, and development on wildlife— including raptors in the northeastern portion of the NPR–A, identified the need for current distributional information on raptors in that region. It is important to note that the status and abundance of at least one species, the peregrine falcon, had changed substantially in northern Alaska since the 1977 survey (Ambrose et al. 1988). However, with the exception of annual monitoring of peregrines along the main Colville River, information from other areas in the NPR–A was scant, incomplete, outdated, or limited in accessibility (unpublished agency trip reports). The objectives of this study were to (1) duplicate, as closely as possible, aerial survey coverage and techniques employed in 1977 to compare cliff-nesting raptor populations between the two periods; (2) assess the present distribution, abundance, and degree of recovery of the peregrine falcon population in the region; and (3) identify and assess cliff-nesting habitats in areas not previously surveyed in the northeastern portion of the NPR–A.

Peregrine falcons are emphasized in this report because of the role they have played in influencing the development of protection strategies for all raptors in northern Alaska, their special status (i.e., recently delisted endangered species), and because of dramatic increases in their populations recorded in other regions of northern Alaska (Ambrose et al. 1988).

Photo by Jim Silva, Bureau of Land Management.

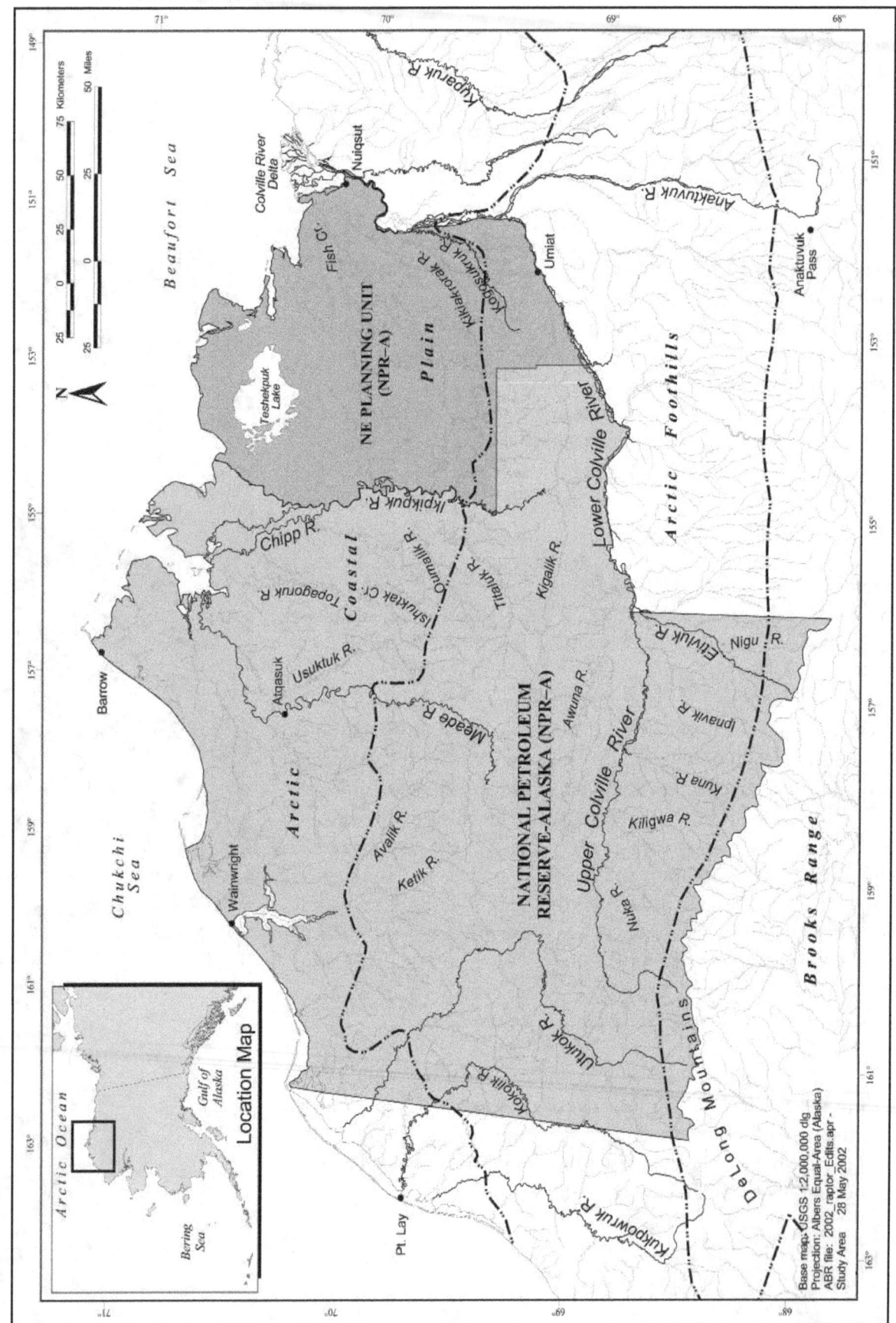

Figure 1. Map of the National Petroleum Reserve–Alaska showing the Northeast Planning Unit and major drainages surveyed for raptors. (The dashed lines delineate the three ecoregions: the Arctic Coastal Plain, the Arctic Foothills, and the Brooks Range.)

Study Area

The 1999 study area generally included all cliff habitats in the NPR–A, excluding the Kogosukruk and Kikiakrorak Rivers and the Colville River below its junction with the Etivluk River (Figures 1 and 2). This area is composed of three ecoregions (Figure 1): Arctic Coastal Plain, Arctic Foothills, and Brooks Range (including the De Long Mountains; Gallant et al. 1996). Figure 2 shows a comparison of the areas surveyed in 1977 and 1999.

Ritchie (1979) described six habitats used for nesting substrates by cliff-nesting raptors in the Arctic Foothills and Brooks Range ecoregions of the NPR–A: shale banks, mud (soil) or sand banks, rock cliffs (along floodplains), outcrops (isolated rock exposures, removed from floodplains), scree and talus slopes, and escarpment faces (extensive cliffs associated with large, off-river mesas; Appendix B). These habitat types were used during the present study to describe areas in the NE Planning Unit not previously mapped.

The Arctic Coastal Plain is the northernmost ecoregion, bounded by the Arctic Ocean and characterized by little topographical relief and low-gradient, meandering watercourses. Consequently, habitats are limited for cliff-nesting raptors. However, a few landforms in this region (i.e., pingoes [ice-cored hills or mounds], coastal bluffs, and dunes and mud banks along lake shorelines and some meandering rivers) offer potential habitat for cliff-nesting raptors—particularly peregrine falcons and rough-legged hawks.

Most habitats for cliff-nesting raptors in the NPR–A occur in the Arctic Foothills ecoregion. This wide swath of rolling hills and plateaus, formed by the gentle warping of sedimentary beds into anticlines and synclines, grades from the Arctic Coastal Plain on the north to the Brooks Range on the south. Cliff habitat has been created in many areas where streams have crossed and eroded the geologic folds. The area can be separated into northern and southern sections. The northern section is dominated by loosely consolidated cutbanks (<600 m in elevation) and the southern section (<800 m in elevation) includes rock outcrops along fast, braided rivers and off-river sites

Photo by Jim Silva, Bureau of Land Management.

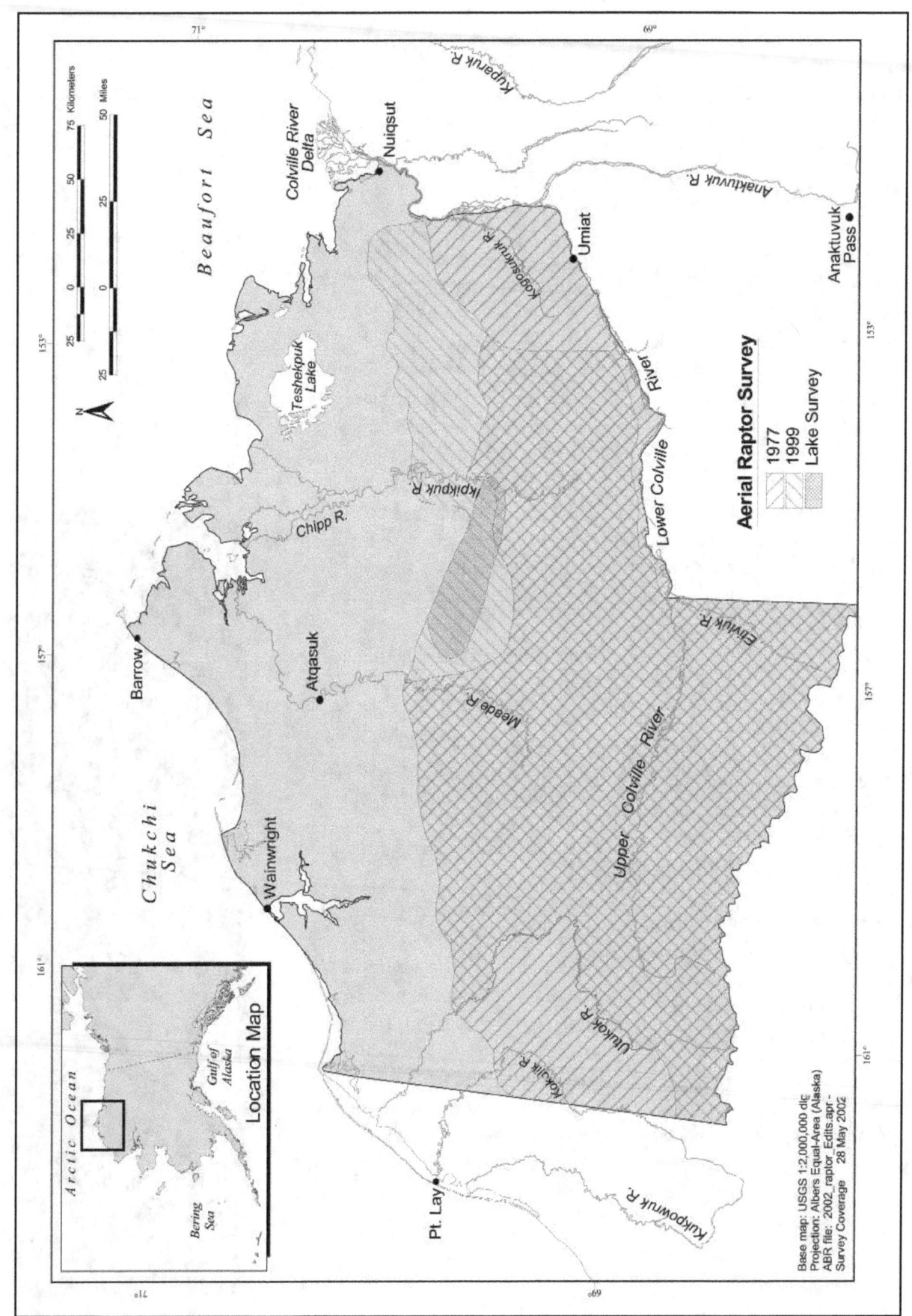

Figure 2. Comparison of the areas surveyed in 1977 and 1999, including a region of lakes surveyed in 1999 (near center of map).

on cliffs and rock outcrops associated with mesas and buttes (Gallant et al. 1996).

The Brooks Range ecoregion generally comprises several rugged mountain areas, including cliffs, in the western Brooks Range and De Long Mountains of the NPR–A. These areas provide nest sites for cliff-nesting raptors, particularly golden eagles and gyrfalcons. Most of this ecoregion in the NPR–A is dominated by talus and scree slopes, however, which are poor habitats for cliff-nesting raptors. Furthermore, because cliff habitats in this ecogregion exceed general elevation limits for nesting by peregrine falcons (Cade 1960), they provide limited opportunities for peregrines.

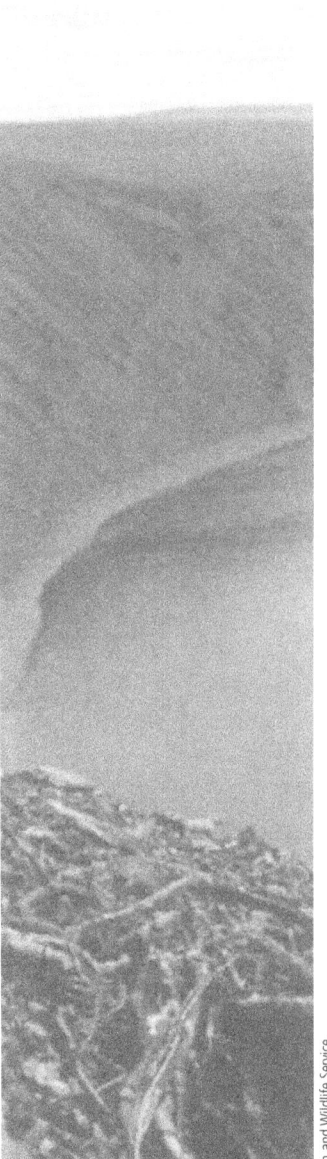

Methods

Aerial surveys were conducted in the NPR–A between 23 and 29 July and on 2 August 1999. In 1977, aerial surveys were flown between 27 June and 11 July (Ritchie 1979), or about 2 to 3 weeks earlier than surveys in 1999. This difference in survey timing (i.e., 1977 surveys occurred earlier in the breeding cycle) needs to be considered when comparing results of the 2 years.

A Piper Super Cub fixed-wing aircraft with a pilot and one observer was used for all surveys. Standard operating procedures involved flying at 120 kph and <200 m above ground level along drainages, ridgelines, and other areas where bank and cliff exposures suitable for nesting occurred. When suitable habitats were identified, we made slower (80 kph) passes at lateral distances of about 50 m. Multiple passes (two to four) were often required to better determine occupancy and productivity, particularly where cliffs were large or complex. Except where tight maneuvering was hazardous because of the topography (e.g., invaginated cliffs), nesting habitats were approached as directly as possible to minimize surprising nesting birds (Fyfe and Olendorff 1976). In addition to limitations imposed by terrain, some cliffs could not be approached closely because of locally unsafe winds or the proximity of defensive and aggressive adults.

At each suitable nesting habitat we searched for signs of raptor use, including the presence of stick nests and nesting ledges, whitewash (feces) deposits, and the presence of adult raptors or young. The following information was recorded at each site where at least one individual raptor was recorded or a definitive sign of raptor nesting use (e.g., stick nest, nest ledge) was identified:

Unique site number (sequential for each U.S. Geological Survey [USGS] 1:250,000 map);

Location (recorded on USGS 1:250,000 map);

Latitude and longitude (World Geodetic System 1984 [WGS-84] datum; recorded with onboard global positioning system [GPS]);

Species present were the peregrine falcon, gyrfalcon, golden eagle, and rough-legged hawk; common raven (*Corvus corax*) nests were also noted, although this species was not a target of this study. At some sites only young were recorded and the

Photo by Bruce Durtsche, Bureau of Land Management.

species was determined by a combination of factors such as plumage (e.g., white down of falcons vs. gray [second] down in rough-legged hawks), nest type (e.g., large, regularly inaccessible stick nest of golden eagle vs. smaller, often more accessible hawk nest), and expected nest phenology differences (e.g., most gyrfalcons were fledged or nearly fledged vs. midnestling stage of peregrine falcons in late July) among species. If nests or nestlings could not be identified as to species, they were described as "unknown";

Number of adults (pairs were counted for sites where young were present); number and approximate age of young; presence of eggs;

Occupancy: (1) Unoccupied—nest present but no adults observed; could include nests used before 1999; (2) Occupied—pair of adults or an aggressive single adult, in combination with other signs of use (e.g., nest); and (3) Occupied and Successful—at least one young present or recently fledged;

Dimensions of the nesting habitat (e.g., height and length of cliffs) and height of nest in meters; (Estimated from the aircraft; these were crude estimations intended to provide a rough idea of the relative size of the substrate);

General habitat category as defined in Ritchie (1979): shale banks, mud (also described as soil in this report) or sand banks, rock cliffs (along floodplains), outcrops (isolated rock exposures, removed from floodplains), scree and talus slopes, and escarpment faces (cliffs associated with large, off-river mesas);

Location of riverine site on left or right bank when facing upstream; and

Primary exposure of cliff and nest (nearest 45 degrees).

Productivity values are presented for successful pairs and for all pairs. The values of young per pair for all pairs, however, are probably artificially high and should be used with caution. We conducted only one survey, whereas two surveys are essential for improving the accuracy of this calculation (Steenof 1987). That is, many pairs that did not nest or had failed nests probably departed their territories before the time of our survey, resulting in an inflated estimation of young per pair for all pairs according to our counts. Nonetheless, the calculations are included in the present report because they allow a gross comparison with other studies reporting this value.

After surveys were completed, GPS location data were entered on GIS base maps with Atlas-GIS Software (ESRI, Redlands, California).

Results

Survey Conditions and Limitations

In the Brooks Range and Arctic Foothills ecoregions of the NPR–A, nearly all major drainages and their tributaries, as well as intervening off-river rock outcrops and ridges surveyed in 1977, were resurveyed for raptors in 1999 (Figure 2). Mid- to upriver portions of major streams on the Arctic Coastal Plain, however—especially those with their origins in the Foothills between the Meade and Colville Rivers—were surveyed more extensively in 1999 than in 1977. Also during the 1999 flights, a number of lakes with steep, eroding soil banks (>5 m in height), were noted in a transitional area between the northern edge of the Arctic Foothills and the southern edge of the Arctic Coastal Plain. A sample of these lakes was surveyed, primarily those between the Ikpikpuk and Titaluk Rivers, including the Oumalik Lakes area (Figure 2).

The Kokolik River and its tributaries and portions of the Utukok, the Kogosukruk, and Kikiakrorak Rivers in the Arctic Foothills ecoregion were not surveyed in 1999. Dangerous winds thwarted attempts to fly the entire Utukok and Kokolik drainages. However, these two rivers were surveyed by Peter Bente (Alaska Department of Fish and Game [ADFG], personal communication; Appendix A) during the late incubation to early nestling stage (4–9 July 1999), and we summarize here some of his observations. We did not survey the Kogosukruk and Kikiakrorak Rivers because a complete helicopter survey of these rivers was conducted in 1997 (T. Swem, U.S. Fish and Wildlife Service [USFWS], personal communication; Appendix A) that provided sufficient information for describing present raptor use. Similarly, the main Colville River, below its junction with the Etivluk River, was not included in this survey because it was surveyed by boat in 1999 (T. Swem, USFWS, personal communication; Appendix A).

Peregrine Falcons

Peregrine falcons occupied 67 sites in the NPR–A in 1999 (Table 1). These sites were composed of a minimum of 51 pairs and 16 single adults. Most (84%) of the pairs observed were successful, producing at least one young. For the entire study area, productivity averaged 2.3 young per successful pair (Table 1) and 2.0 young per pair for all pairs (Table 2).

Photo courtesy of the Bureau of Land Management.

Table 1. Distribution, abundance, and productivity of peregrine falcons (*Falco peregrinus tundrius*) by river drainage in the National Petroleum Reserve–Alaska, 1999.

Drainage	All Sites	Single Adults	Pairs	Successful Pairs	Young	Young per Successful Pair
Avalik	2	0	2	2	6	3.0
Awuna	0	0	0	0		
Colville, Upper	9	1	8	7	18	2.6
Etivluk	2	0	2	1	2	2.0
Fish Creek	9	3	6	6	14	2.3
Ikpikpuk	5	2	13	12	29	2.4
Ipnavik	2	0	2	1	1	1.0
Ishuktak	2	1	1	1	2	2.0
Ketik	0	0	0	0		
Kigalik	1	0	1	1	1	1.0
Kiligwa	3	1	2	2	6	3.0
Kokolik	0	0	0	0		
Kuna	1	1	0	0		
Meade	0	0	0	0		
Nigu	0	0	0	0		
Nuka	0	0	0	0		
Oumalik Lakes	4	1	3	3	3	1.0
Oumalik River	1	1	0	0		
Titaluk	5	2	3	2	6	3.0
Topagoruk	4	1	3	2	7	3.5
Usuktuk	2	1	1	1	1	1.0
Utukok	5	1	4	2	4	2.0
Total	67	16	51	43	100	2.3

Most peregrine falcon sites (61%) were found in a narrow belt of low-relief tundra drained by meandering, slow-gradient rivers north of the Colville River (Figure 3), including the Ikpikpuk River and its primary tributaries, the Titaluk and Price Rivers, and Fry Creek. The area is rich in lakes, which are often bordered at their northern ends by rolling-to-steep exposed soil banks, caused by thermokarsting (erosion). Peregrines (three pairs, two of which were successful, and two single adults) were located at five lakes in this region (Figure 4). Additionally, a few sites (6%) were located in the northern Foothills and the rest (33%) were distributed in the lower reaches of the Colville tributaries that drain the northern side of the Brooks Range (Table 2).

Peregrine falcons primarily nested on low mud and sand banks (69%) associated with low-gradient streams and lakes in a transitional zone between the Arctic Coastal Plain and northern Foothills, or shale bluffs (27%) associated with faster braided streams in the southern Foothills (Table 3a). Rock cliffs and scree slopes were also used to a limited degree. All sites were closely associated with riverine or lacustrine (i.e., deep, open lakes) habitats. No pairs or single birds were recorded at off-river rock outcrops. The mean elevation of nest sites with pairs was 174 m (SD = 144; range 30–490 m; n = 51; Table 3a). Approximate dimensions of nest site substrates used by peregrine falcons are summarized in Table 3b.

Photo by Alexander Reshetniak, Raptor Education Foundation.

Table 2. Distribution, abundance, and productivity of cliff-nesting raptors in 1977 and 1999 in ecoregions of the National Petroleum Reserve–Alaska, 1999.

Ecoregion	Peregrine Falcon *(Falco peregrinus tundrius)*				Gyrfalcon *(Falco rusticolus)*			
	All Sites	Pairs	Young	Young per pair	All Sites	Pairs	Young	Young per pair
1977								
Coastal Plain	0	0	0		1	1	0	0
Northern Foothills	1	0	0		7	4	7	1.8
Southern Foothills and Brooks Range	2	2	0	0	21	16	27	1.7
Total	3	2	0	0	29	21	34	1.6
1999								
Coastal Plain	41	29	60	2.1	2	1	3	3.0
Northern Foothills	4	4	9	2.3	5	4	7	1.8
Southern Foothills and Brooks Range	22	18	31	1.7	34	11	15	1.4
Total	67	51	100	2.0	41	16	25	1.6

[a] ND = not detected; survey in 1977 mostly confined to incubation stage, and limited numbers of young could be detected.

	Golden Eagle				Rough-legged Hawk[a]			
	(*Aquila chrysaetos*)				(*Buteo lagopus*)			
	All Sites	Pairs	Young	Young per pair	All Sites	Pairs	Young	Young per pair
	0	0	0		1	1	ND	ND
	0	0	0		15	13	ND	ND
	25	10	17	1.7	44	41	ND	ND
	25	10	17	1.7	60	55	ND	ND
	0	0	0		7	7	14	2.0
	0	0	0		30	18	35	1.9
	35	11	13	1.2	145	84	161	1.9
	35	11	13	1.2	182	109	210	1.9

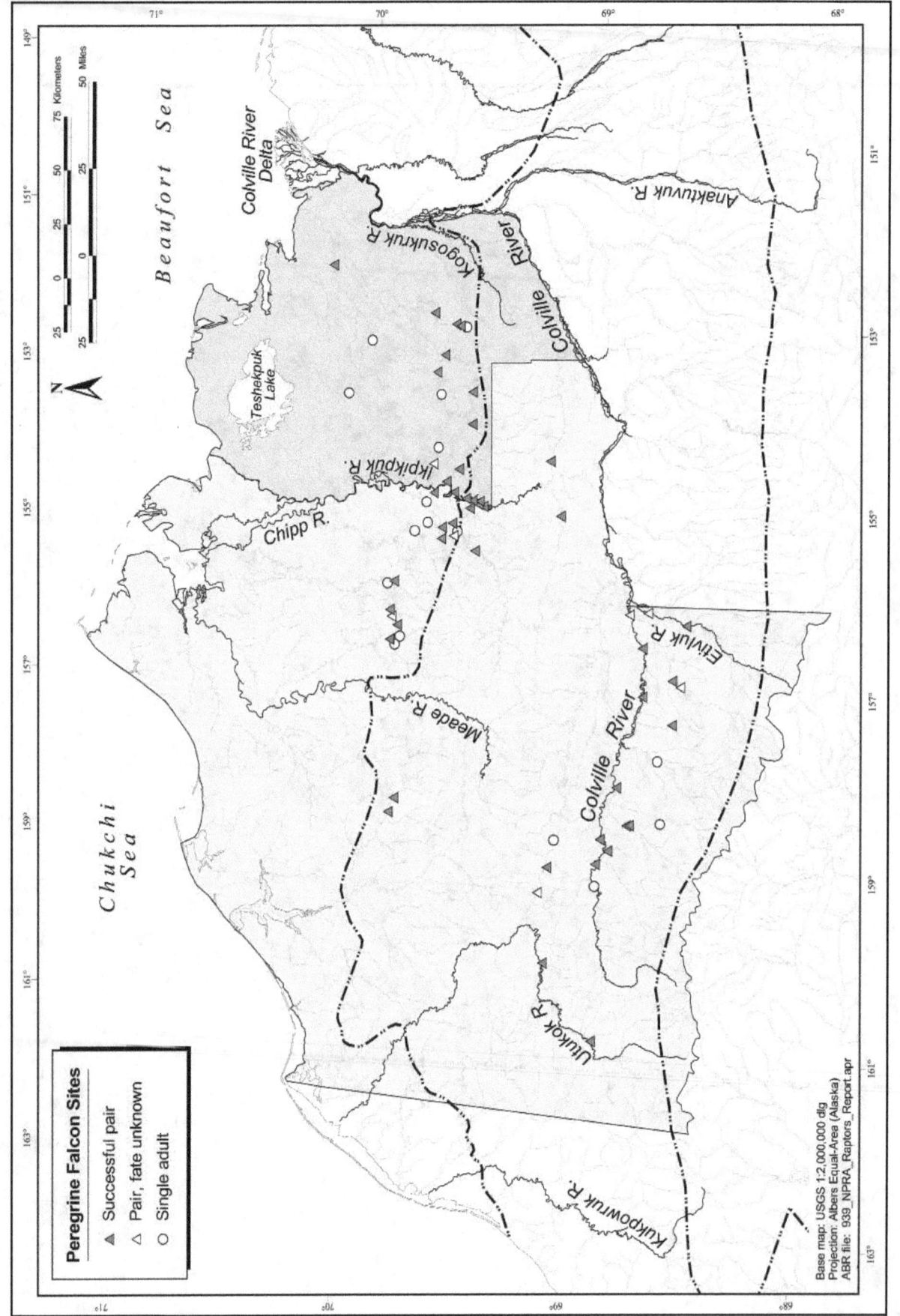

Figure 3. Distribution of peregrine falcon (*Falco peregrinus tundrius*) sites identified during fixed-wing aerial surveys in the National Petroleum Reserve–Alaska, July 1999. (The dashed lines delineate the three ecoregions: the Arctic Coastal Plain, the Arctic Foothills, and the Brooks Range [see Figure 1].)

Peregrine Falcon Sites
▲ Successful pair
△ Pair, fate unknown
○ Single adult

Base map: USGS 1:2,000,000 dlg
Projection: Albers Equal-Area (Alaska)
ABR file: 939_NPRA_Raptors_Report.apr

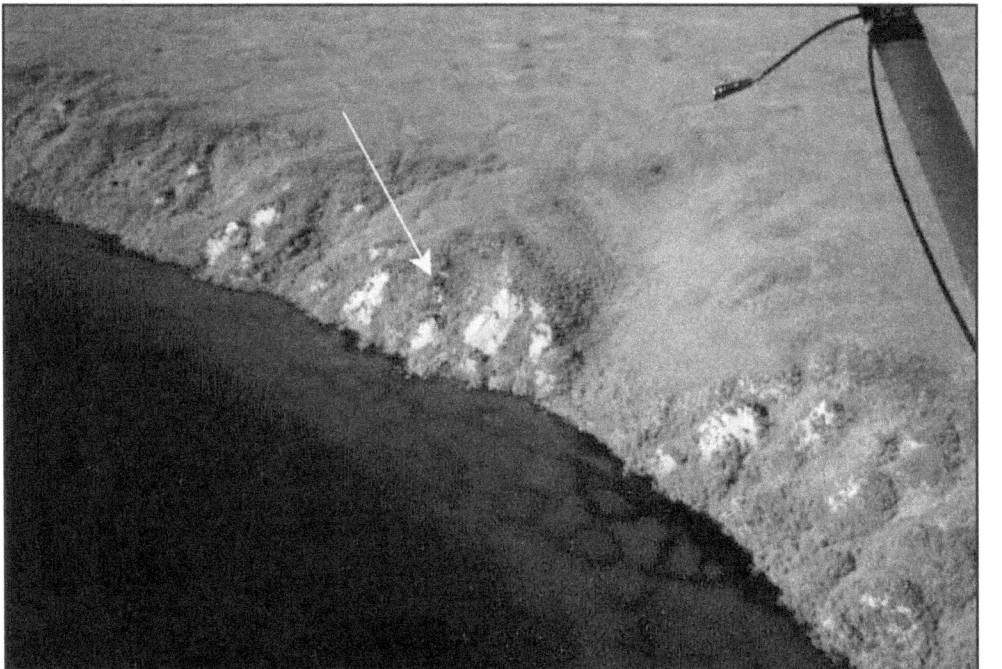

Figure 4. Photographs of (*a*) mud bank habitat on a large lake in the Oumalik Lakes area, northern Alaska; and (*b*) a portion of that bank used by peregrine falcons (*Falco peregrinus tundrius*) for nesting.

Table 3a. Frequency (proportions) of use of different substrate types and mean elevation (in meters) of nest sites of peregrine falcons (*Falco peregrinus tundrius*), gyrfalcons (*Falco rusticolus*), golden eagles (*Aquila chrysaetos*), and rough-legged hawks (*Buteo lagopus*) in the National Petroleum Reserve–Alaska, 1999.

Species	n		Escarpment		Mud Bank		Rock Outcrop (floodplain)	
	All Sites	Pairs	All Sites	Pairs	All Sites	Pairs	All Sites	Pairs
Peregrine Falcon	67	51	0	0	0.70	0.69	0.03	0.02
Gyrfalcon	41	16	0.10	0.06	0.02	0	0.76	0.69
Golden Eagle	35	11	0.03	0.09	0	0	0.83	0.82
Rough-legged Hawk	182	109	0.01	0.02	0.10	0.11	0.26	0.24

Table 3b. Estimated dimensions of substrates at sites used by peregrine falcons (*Falco peregrinus tundrius*), gyrfalcons (*Falco rusticolus*), golden eagles (*Aquila chrysaetos*), and rough-legged hawks (*Buteo lagopus*) in the National Petroleum Reserve–Alaska, 1999.

		All Sites								
Species	n	Height (m)			Length (m)			Nest Height (m)		
		mean	SD	range	mean	SD	range	mean	SD	range
Peregrine Falcon	67	26	12	5–75	156	91	20–400	20	10	4–48
Gyrfalcon	41	43	30	7–150	130	139	20–800	25	16	3–75
Golden Eagle	35	53	28	10–125	138	157	20–800	33	20	7–90
Rough-legged Hawk	182	22	13	5–80	88	71	10–400	14	8	1–45

Rock Outcrop (nonfloodplain)		Shale Bank		Scree Slope		Elevation (m)					
						All Sites			Pairs		
All Sites	Pairs	All Sites	Pairs	All Sites	Pairs	mean	SD	range	mean	SD	range
0	0	0.25	0.27	0.01	0.02	169	146	30–490	174	144	30–490
0	0	0.12	0.25	0	0	398	201	60–730	368	203	60–670
0	0	0.06	0	0.09	0.09	597	162	150–820	615	173	180–790
0.02	0.02	0.43	0.48	0.17	0.14	364	163	30–730	364	157	30–670

	Pairs								
n	Height (m)			Length (m)			Nest Height (m)		
	mean	SD	range	mean	SD	range	mean	SD	range
51	27	10	8–50	152	79	20–400	20	10	4–48
16	36	26	7–100	159	194	25–800	22	14	3–50
11	47	19	20–75	155	227	30–800	30	14	17–60
109	24	12	5–80	91	61	15–400	16	8	1–45

Table 4. Distribution, abundance, and productivity of gyrfalcons (*Falco rusticolus*) by river drainage in the National Petroleum Reserve–Alaska, 1999.

Drainage	All Sites	Single Adults	Pairs	Successful Pairs	Young	Young per Successful Pair
Avalik	0	0	0	0		
Awuna	2	0	2	2	4	2.0
Colville, Upper	3	0	3	3	6	2.0
Etivluk	1	0	1	0		
Fish Creek	0	0	0	0		
Ikpikpuk	2	0	0	0		
Ipnavik	2	0	0	0		
Ishuktak	0	0	0	0		
Ketik	0	0	0	0		
Kigalik	1	0	1	1	2	2.0
Kiligwa	5	0	2	2	2	1.0
Kokolik	0	0	0	0		
Kuna	8	0	2	2	3	1.5
Meade	1	0	1	1	1	1.0
Nigu	3	0	0	0		
Nuka	1	0	1	1	2	2.0
Oumalik Lakes	0	0	0	0		
Oumalik River	0	0	0	0		
Titaluk	1	0	1	1	3	3.0
Topagoruk	0	0	0	0		
Usuktuk	0	0	0	0		
Utukok	11	3	2	2	2[a]	2.0
Total	41	3	16	15	25	1.8

[a] The number of young was only determined at one of two successful sites on the Utukok River.

Gyrfalcons

Forty-one sites or cliff locations (characteristically whitewash [feces]-covered nest ledges or ledges with adults or young present) probably used by gyrfalcons were identified during our aerial surveys in the NPR–A (Table 4). Many of these locations may not have been occupied in 1999. The timing of our surveys did not allow a determination of occupancy at many sites. Gyrfalcons occupied 19 of these sites, including 3 single adults and 16 pairs, whereas 22 sites were unoccupied. Most pairs (93%) were successful, and for the entire study area productivity averaged 1.8 young per successful pair (Table 4) and 1.6 young per pair for all pairs (Table 2). Because we probably missed identifying some young because of the timing of our aerial survey (i.e., our surveys were flown after some gyrfalcons had already fledged), productivity values may be higher.

Most gyrfalcon nest sites (83%) were on cliffs in the southern Foothills, particularly in the southwestern portion of the study area (Figure 5); sites on the Kiligwa, Kuna, and Utukok Rivers accounted for more than half (58%) of all recorded sites (Table 4). This area has the most well-developed cliff faces—both riparian and off-river—and relatively steep-gradient braided rivers cutting through moist tussock and alpine tundra. In contrast, only seven sites were located in the northern Foothills and its transition with the Arctic Coastal Plain (Table 2).

Gyrfalcons primarily nested on rock cliffs (69%) and shale banks (25%) associated with the floodplains of rivers in the Arctic Foothills (Table 3a). A few sites (6%) were on off-river outcrops and on escarpment cliffs in the southern Foothills. No pairs were recorded on scree and talus slopes or on unconsolidated soil or mud banks often found in the northern Foothills and Coastal Plain, respectively. The mean elevation of nest sites with pairs was 368 m (SD = 203 m; range 60–670 m; n = 16; Table 3a). Gyrfalcons generally used larger cliff habitats than peregrine falcons and rough-legged hawks (Table 3b).

Photo by Ted Swem, U.S. Fish and Wildlife Service.

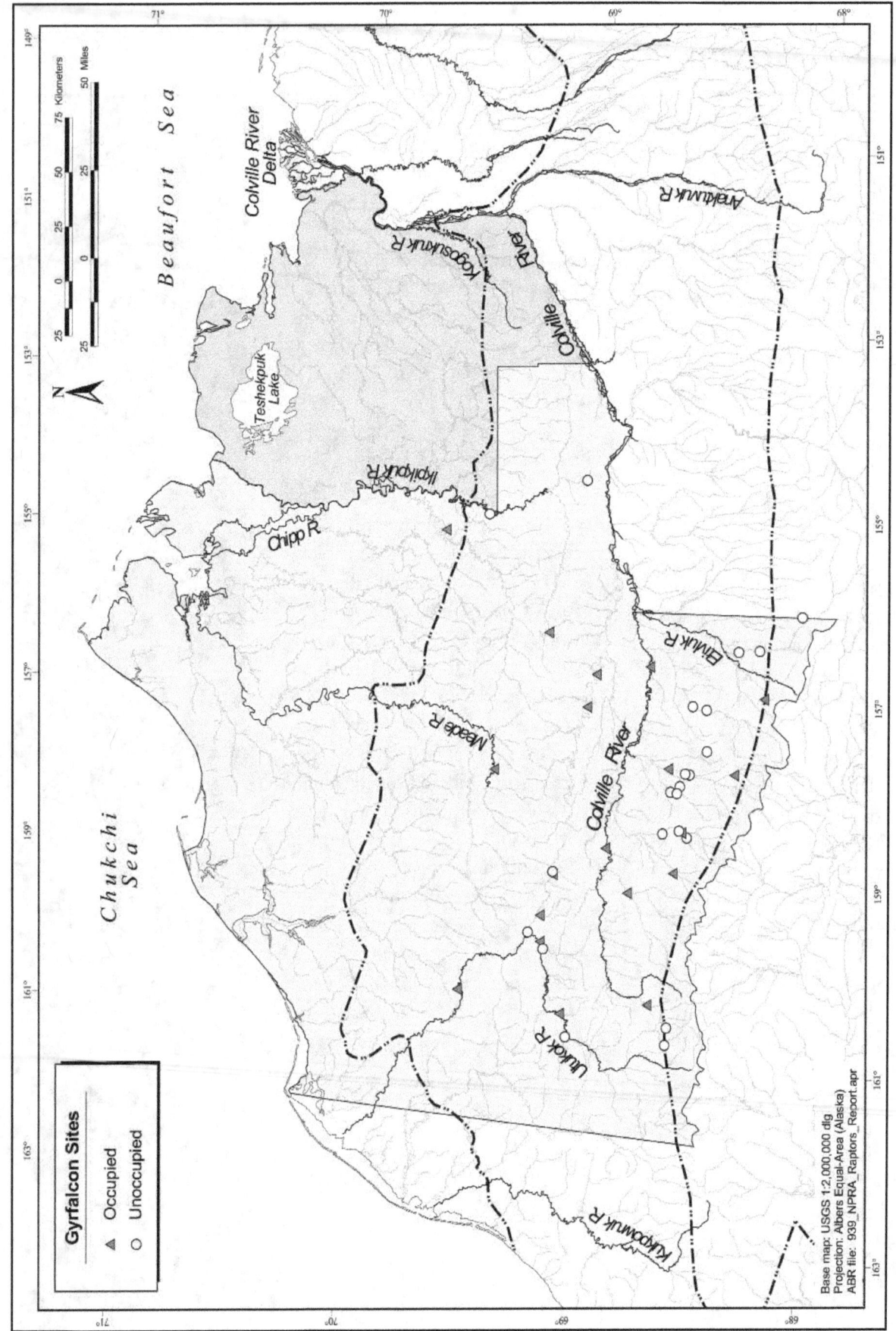

Figure 5. Distribution of gyrfalcon (*Falco rusticolus*) sites identified during fixed-wing aerial surveys in the National Petroleum Reserve–Alaska, July 1999. (The dashed lines delineate the three ecoregions: the Arctic Coastal Plain, the Arctic Foothills, and the Brooks Range [see Figure 1].)

Golden Eagles

We identified (by the presence of stick nests, adults, or young) 35 cliff locations that golden eagles had used for nesting during our aerial surveys in the NPR–A (Table 5). Many of these locations were probably not used in 1999, and some represent alternative nest sites for pairs nesting at other locations. Golden eagles occupied at least 12 of these sites, including 11 successful pairs and a single adult. Productivity averaged 1.2 young per successful pair (Table 5; same for all pairs, Table 2) for the entire study area.

In the southern Foothills, golden eagle nest sites were distributed in the same drainages, and golden eagles used substrate types similar to those used by gyrfalcons (i.e., generally large, vertical face cliffs; Tables 2 and 3a, Figure 6). Nests on the Kiligwa, Kuna, and Utukok Rivers accounted for nearly three-fourths (71%) of all observed nests (Table 5). The southern Foothills have the most well-developed cliff faces, both on and off relatively steep-gradient, braided rivers that cut through moist tussock and alpine tundra.

Golden eagles usually nested (82%) on the largest cliffs that were associated with rivers in the southern Foothills near the Brooks Range (Table 3a and b). A few sites were off-river on escarpment cliffs (9%) or on talus slopes along rivers (9%). Although no pairs or sites were identified on unconsolidated soil or mud banks in the northern Foothills or Arctic Coastal Plain, subadult eagles regularly were observed in these areas. The mean elevation of nest sites with pairs was 615 m (SD = 173 m; range 180–790 m; n = 11). The lowest elevation nests were on the Utukok River.

Table 5. Distribution, abundance, and productivity of golden eagles (*Aquila chrysaetos*) by river drainage in the National Petroleum Reserve–Alaska, 1999.

Drainage	All Sites	Single Adults	Pairs	Successful Pairs	Young	Young per Successful Pair
Avalik	0	0	0	0		
Awuna	0	0	0	0		
Colville, Upper	2	0	2	2	2	1.0
Etivluk	0	0	0	0		
Fish Creek	0	0	0	0		
Ikpikpuk	0	0	0	0		
Ipnavik	3	0	1	1	2	2.0
Ishuktak	0	0	0	0		
Ketik	0	0	0	0		
Kigalik	0	0	0	0		
Kiligwa	8	0	2	2	3	1.5
Kokolik	2	1	1	1	1	1.0
Kuna	5	0	1	1	1	1.0
Meade	0	0	0	0		
Nigu	1	0	0	0		
Nuka	2	0	0	0		
Oumalik Lakes	0	0	0	0		
Oumalik River	0	0	0	0		
Titaluk	0	0	0	0		
Topagoruk	0	0	0	0		
Usuktuk	0	0	0	0		
Utukok	12	0	4	4	4	1.0
Total	35	1	11	11	13	1.2

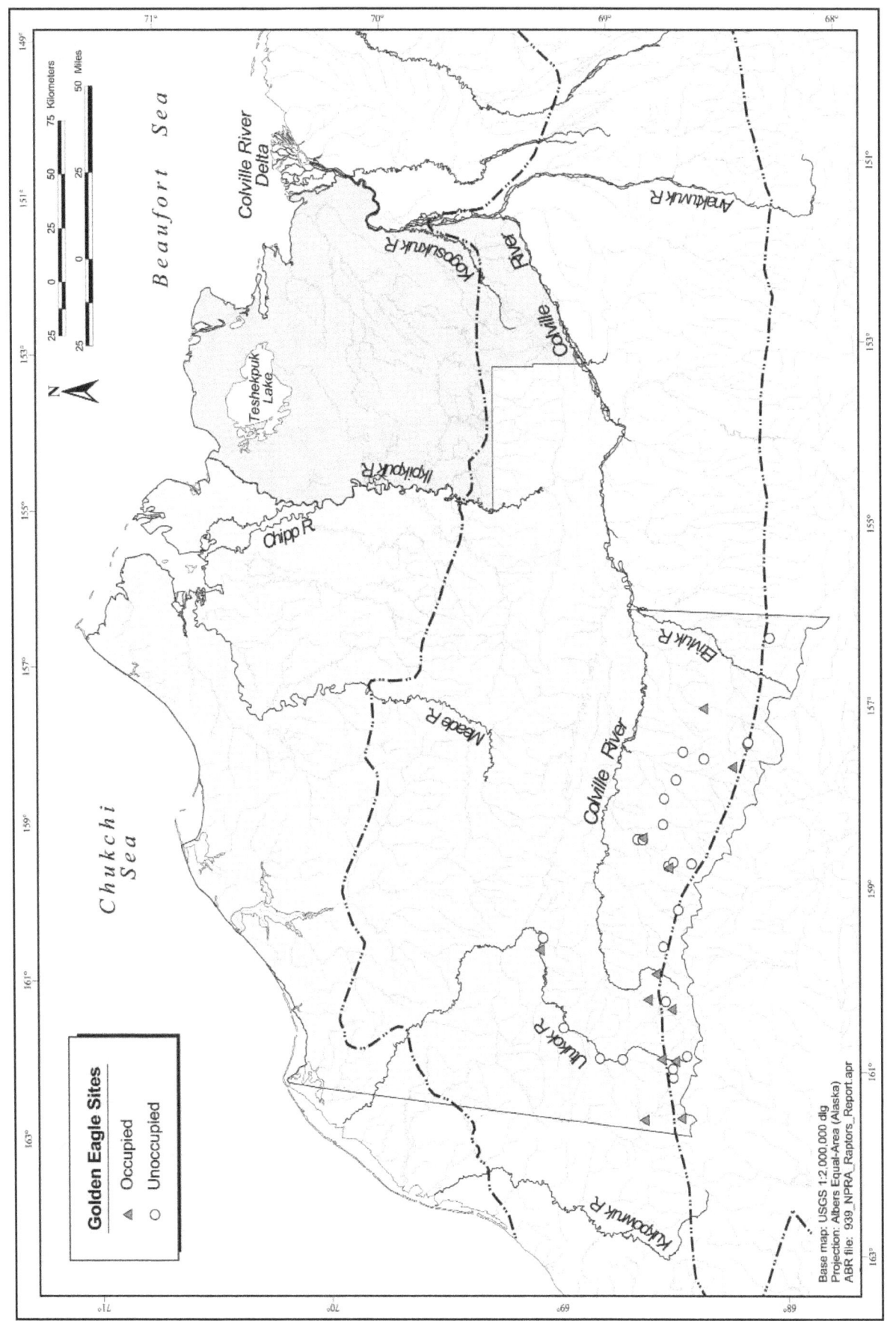

Figure 6. Distribution of golden eagle (*Aquila chrysaetos*) sites identified during fixed-wing aerial surveys in the National Petroleum Reserve–Alaska, July 1999. (The dashed lines delineate the three ecoregions: the Arctic Coastal Plain, the Arctic Foothills, and the Brooks Range [see Figure 1].)

Table 6. Distribution, abundance, and productivity of rough-legged hawks *(Buteo lagopus)* by river drainage in the National Petroleum Reserve–Alaska, 1999.

Drainage	All Sites	Single Adults	Pairs	Successful Pairs	Young	Young per Successful Pair
Avalik	3	0	1	1	1	1.0
Awuna	9	1	6	6	11	1.8
Colville, Upper	24	1	16	16	29	1.8
Etivluk	14	2	9	9	20	2.2
Fish Creek	2	0	2	2	3	1.5
Ikpikpuk	7	0	4	4	8	2.0
Ipnavik	22	0	13	12	26	2.2
Ishuktak	1	0	1	1	3	3.0
Ketik	1	0	0	0		
Kigalik	6	0	5	5	12	2.4
Kiligwa	12	0	8	7	13	1.9
Kokolik	2	0	2	2	3	1.5
Kuna	15	2	10	10	19	1.9
Meade	7	0	4	4	7	1.8
Nigu	8	0	3	3	6	2.0
Nuka	8	1	4	4	8	2.0
Oumalik Lakes	0	0	0	0		
Oumalik River	0	0	0	0		
Titaluk	2	0	2	2	4	2.0
Topagoruk	0	0	0	0		
Usuktuk	0	0	0	0		
Utukok	39	4	19	18	37	2.1
Total	182	11	109	106	210	2.0

Rough-legged Hawks

Rough-legged hawks were the most abundant and widespread cliff-nesting raptors in the NPR–A. We identified 182 locations that had rough-legged hawk nests present (Table 6), of which 66% were occupied. A minimum of 106 nests (88% of occupied sites) were determined to be successful. Young may have fledged from a few nests, limiting our ability to determine the reproductive success of all nests. For the entire study area, productivity averaged 2.0 young per successful pair (Table 6) and 1.9 young per pair for all pairs (Table 2).

Most rough-legged hawk nest sites (80%) were found along cliffs in the southern Foothills (Table 2, Figure 7). Sixty-nine percent of all nests were located on six drainages, including the upper Colville River (Table 6). These same areas were commonly used by golden eagles and gyrfalcons. Rough-legged hawk nests were more sparsely distributed (16%) in the northern Foothills and were only occasionally observed (4%) on the Arctic Coastal Plain.

Rough-legged hawks nested on a wide variety of cliff and bank substrates in the NPR–A (Table 3a). Shale bluffs and rock cliffs were used most often (72%), but scree and talus slopes and mud banks accounted for 25% of sites. A few sites (4%) were off-river on isolated rock outcrops and escarpments in the southern Foothills. The mean elevation of nest sites with pairs was 364 m (SD = 157 m; range 30–670 m; n = 109; Table 3a). The lowest elevation nests were on Fish Creek on the Arctic Coastal Plain. Of the four raptor species surveyed, rough-legged hawks used some of the smallest banks and cliffs available (Table 3b).

Photo by Ted Swem, U.S. Fish and Wildlife Service.

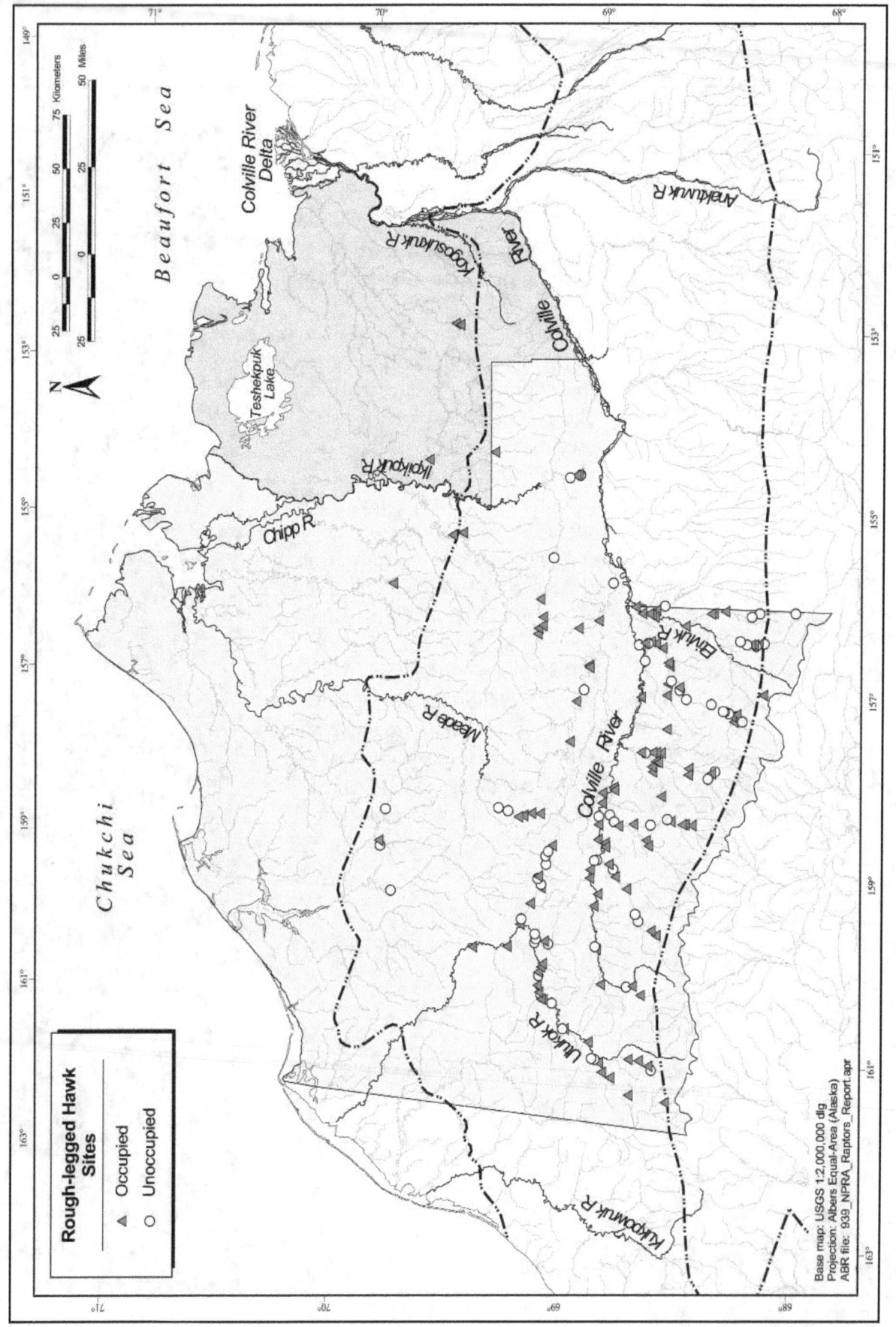

Figure 7. Distribution of rough-legged hawk (*Buteo lagopus*) sites identified during fixed-wing aerial surveys in the National Petroleum Reserve–Alaska, July 1999. (The dashed lines delineate the three ecoregions: the Arctic Coastal Plain, the Arctic Foothills, and the Brooks Range [see Figure 1].)

Nest Site Habitat Assessment

An assessment of suitable nesting habitats for cliff-nesting raptors in most foothill and mountain drainages and their tributaries was made during aerial surveys in 1977 (Ritchie 1979; Appendix B). Habitat values of some areas, particularly the transition zone between the Foothills and Coastal Plain, were only cursorily described in 1977 as poor to fair on the basis of an apparent lack of good nesting substrates. Surveys in 1999, however, were extended farther north than in 1977, particularly in the NE Planning Unit, and this allowed a more thorough appraisal of habitats in this region.

With the exception of a few rock cliffs in the upper reaches of rivers draining from the Foothills, all suitable nesting habitats for cliff-nesting raptors in the NE Planning Unit are sand and mud banks, most of which occur along meandering portions of streams where they exit the Foothills. Habitat descriptions are summarized for these areas (Table 7, Figure 8) according to classifications described in Ritchie (1979). In this area, substrates rarely exceed

25 m and range from 5 to 40 m in height. A few nonvegetated, riverine bluffs and dunes extend onto the Coastal Plain, but do not exceed 15 m in height. Many larger lakes between the Meade and Colville Rivers, especially in the Oumalik and Koluktak Lakes regions, have nesting habitat on steep-banked, primarily south-facing shorelines with partly vegetated soil bluffs 5–20 m high. These lakes occur in a narrow band about 25 km wide along the northern edge of the Arctic Foothills. North of this band are a few more lakes with soil banks, but these are rarely more than 2–3 m high. Similar lake and riparian areas were not surveyed west of the Meade River, but it appears from topographic maps and aerial photos that this type of lacustrine habitat is more limited there than to the east. All of these habitats (lacustrine soil or mud banks and dunes) provide fair-to-good nesting substrates for peregrine falcons, poor-to-fair substrates for rough-legged hawks, and poor substrates for gyrfalcons. Golden eagles regularly use these elevated substrates for perches (Ritchie 1979), but these habitats are not suitable for nesting by this species.

Photo by Ted Swem, U.S. Fish and Wildlife Service.

Table 7. Description of nesting habitat for cliff-nesting raptors in the transition region between the Arctic Foothills and the Arctic Coastal Plain of the Northeast Planning Unit, National Petroleum Reserve–Alaska (areas are mapped in Figure 8). Substrate types: shale banks = SB, Mud or soil banks = MB, rock cliffs = RC, off-river outcrops = O, scree and talus slopes = ST, escarpment faces = EF. Height classes: 1 = >100 m, 2 = 50–100 m, 3 = <50 m (after Ritchie 1979). See Figure 8 for description of habitat assessment values.

Drainage or Area	Substrate Types and Occurrence	Habitat Assessment
Fish Creek	Occasional 3 MBs on Coastal Plain upriver from junction with Judy Creek (<25 m)	III–IV
Inigok Creek	Occasional 3 MBs (<25 m)	III–IV
Key, Judy, Wolf, and Alice Creeks	Scattered 3 MBs (<25 m) between 69° 35' and from Foothills to 69° 47' N in lake transition Coastal Plain; little habitat in Foothills where rolling hills dominant	III–IV
Price River	Occasional 3 MBs with some >25 m	III–IV
Koluktak Lakes	Some small MBs less than 10 m along some deep lake fronts	IV
Oumalik Lakes	Numerous deep lakes with MBs up to 20 m, especially along south side	III–IV
Oumalik River	Limited low soil bluffs (3 MBs)	IV
Ishuktak Creek	MBs between 69° 45' N and 70° 00' N	III–IV
Usuktuk River	A few MBs between 69° 50' N and 70° 00' N	IV
Topagoruk River	A few MBs between 69° 50' N and 70° 00' N	III–IV

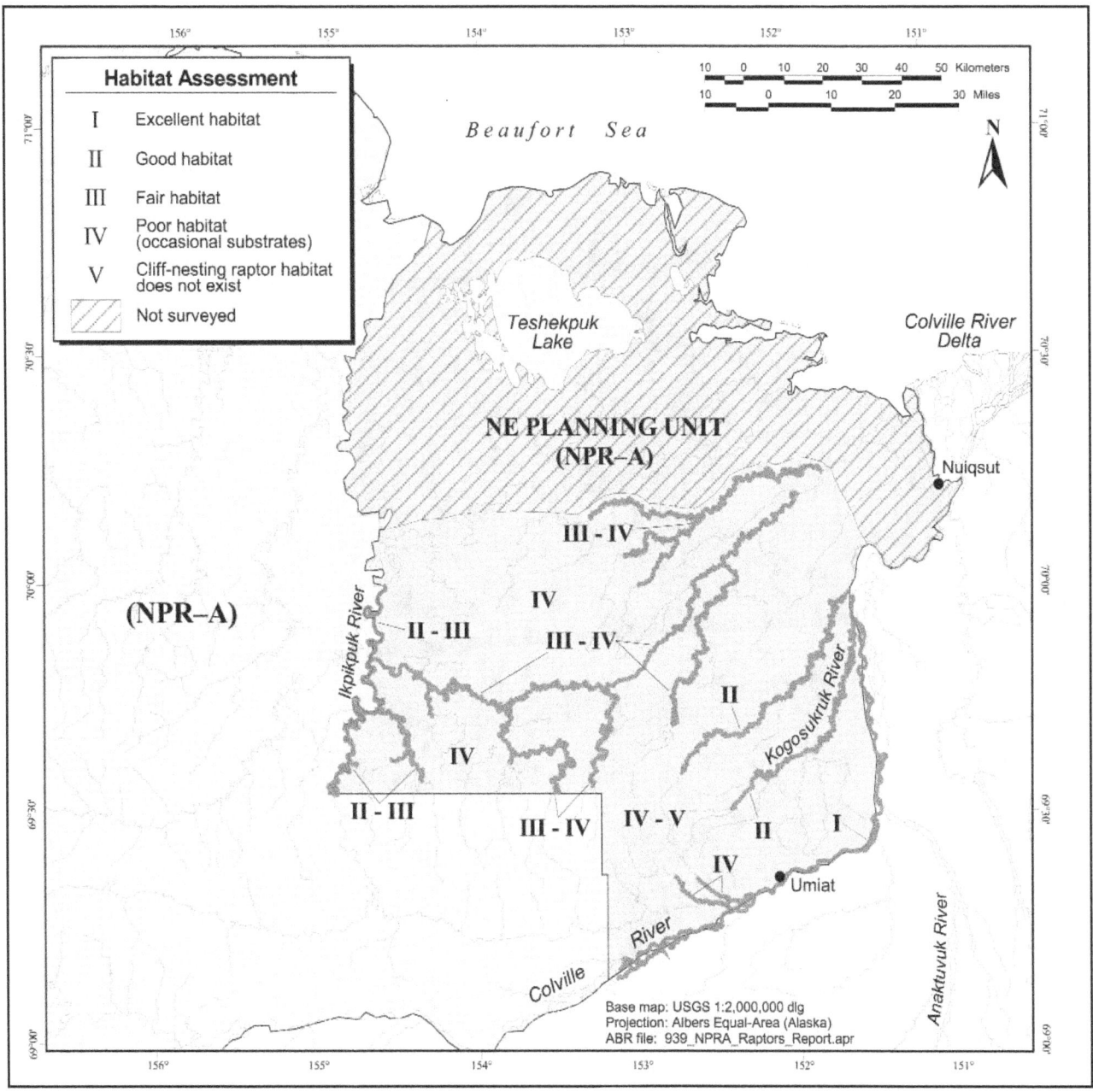

Figure 8. Habitat assessment for cliff-nesting raptors in the Northeast Planning Unit, National Petroleum Reserve–Alaska (additions to mapping found in Ritchie 1979).

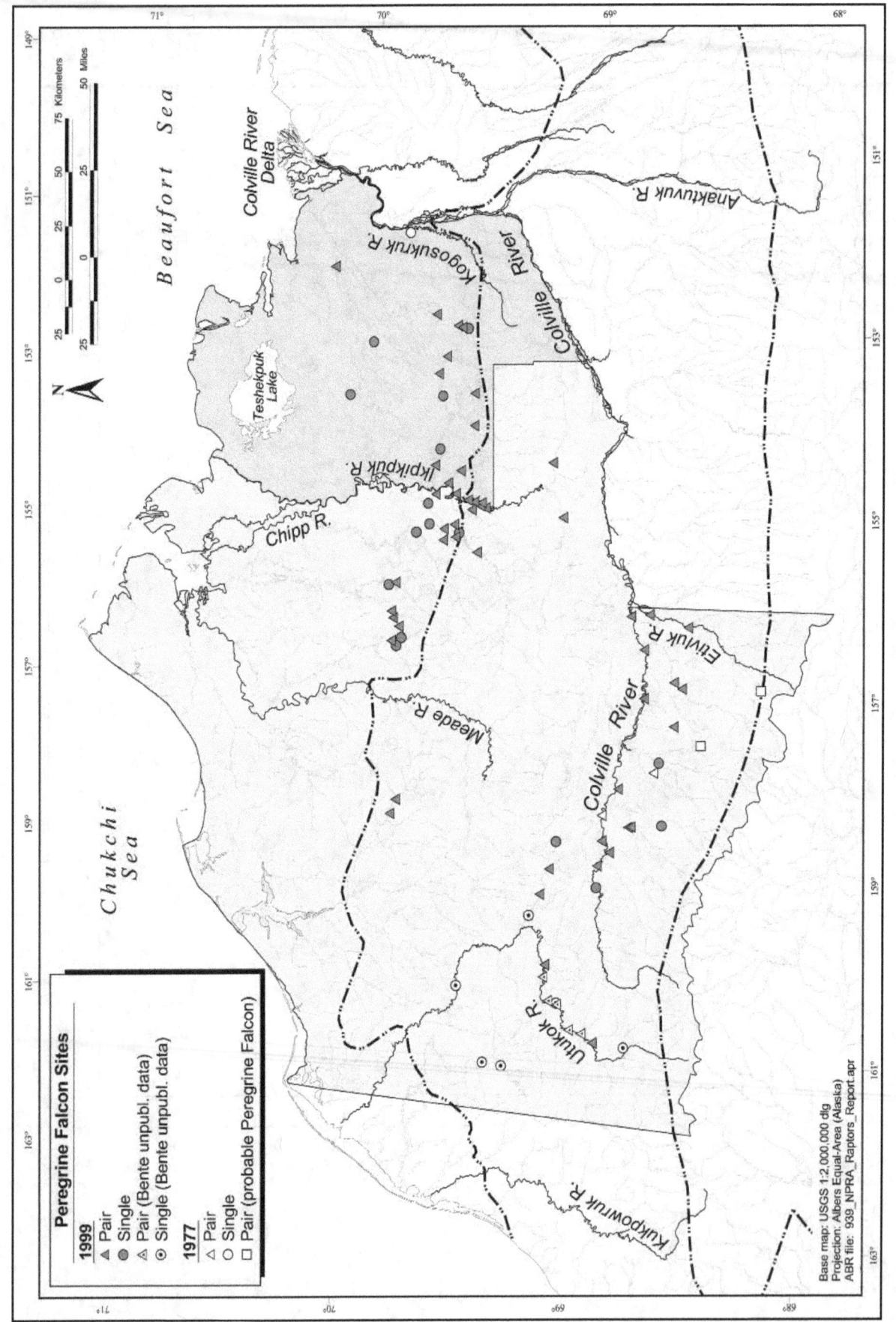

Figure 9. Distribution of peregrine falcon (*Falco peregrinus tundrius*) sites identified during fixed-wing aerial surveys in the National Petroleum Reserve–Alaska, July 1977 and July 1999. Locations are from Ritchie (1977), Bente (1999, unpublished data), and the present study. Excludes sites located on the Colville River below the Etivluk River in all years. (The dashed lines delineate the three ecoregions: the Arctic Coastal Plain, the Arctic Foothills, and the Brooks Range. [see Figure 1].)

Discussion

Peregrine Falcons

A comparison of the 1999 survey with surveys of the 1970s (Pegau 1975; Cade and White 1976; Ritchie 1979) reveals that numbers of peregrine falcons have increased dramatically in the NPR–A (Figure 9). Excluding areas on the Coastal Plain, which were not surveyed in 1977 (about 16 locations with peregrines), and the Kogosukruk and Kikiakrorak Rivers, the number of sites occupied by at least one adult has increased from 4 in 1977 to 61 in 1999. The 1999 total includes 51 sites we identified and an additional 10 sites located during a separate survey on the Utukok and Kokolik Rivers (P. Bente, ADFG, personal communication; Appendix A). The 1977 total includes two dark falcons identified on nests on Fay and Cutaway Creeks (Figure 9). Because these birds were incubating late in the season (not typical of gyrfalcons), and because of the nesting habitats they occupied, they probably were peregrines (Ritchie 1979) and have been included in this total. The two sites that were definitely occupied by peregrines in 1977—a site on the upper Colville River above the mouth of the Kiligwa River (a pair) and a site on Anuk Creek (a single, incubating adult), were revisited in

1999, but only the Colville River site was occupied.

In addition, about 100 pairs of peregrine falcons also occur in other areas of the NPR–A. Surveys conducted on the Kogosukruk and Kikiakrorak Rivers in 1997 identified 28 sites occupied by at least one adult (Swem 1997; Appendix A). Only one site was found occupied by peregrines in 1977 (Ritchie 1979). In addition, the Colville River, below the Etivluk River, had 56 sites occupied by at least one adult peregrine in 1999 (T. Swem, USFWS, personal communication). In 1977, aerial surveys were incomplete along this portion of the Colville River (three occupied sites identified during partial surveys; Ritchie 1979). Finally, our survey did not identify peregrines in some drainages with a recent history of use, such as the Awuna and Nigu Rivers (M. Kunz, BLM, personal communication; Silva and Masinton 1987; Appendix A), suggesting the potential for additional nesting pairs.

Nesting success and productivity of peregrine falcons in the study area exceeded or were within the range of other populations in northern Alaska (Swem 1997; Wright and Bente 1999). In our study area,

Photo by Skip Ambrose, National Park Service.

84% of pairs were successful, compared with 39% and 71% of pairs on the Colville (T. Swem, USFWS, personal communication) and Sagavanirktok (J. Wright, ADFG, personal communication) Rivers, respectively. Productivity for our study was 2.3 young per successful pair, whereas productivity was 2.4 young per successful pair on the main Colville River. Because we were limited to a single visit late in the season, however, our observations were probably biased toward successful pairs (i.e., nonnesting or failed pairs may have departed the area before our survey or were less conspicuous). Two surveys, one during incubation and a second during the nestling stage, are essential for an accurate calculation of nesting success (Steenof 1987).

We were somewhat surprised to locate most peregrine falcon sites in the transitional area between the Arctic Coastal Plains and Arctic Foothills ecoregions and not along the braided drainages of the southern Foothills. This result may partly reflect the lack of surveys conducted during the 1970s in the transitional area, rather than an actual change in distribution. Additionally, this area generally offers more valuable and denser wetland habitats used by primary prey species of peregrine falcons, including

waterfowl and shorebirds, than the foothills region. Indeed, waterbird surveys conducted in the Coastal Plain and Foothills regions have clearly shown greater numbers of ducks and shorebirds, important prey of peregrines, in the transition area than in any areas south (King 1979).

The transitional area is also closer to the densest component of the population (lower Colville, Kogosukruk, and Kikiakrorak Rivers). Greater densities of peregrine falcons in the transitional areas may reflect characteristics of a recovering population if, as peregrines expand, they are occupying habitats closest to their core population centers (i.e., main Colville River). It may be difficult for new pairs to colonize areas farther from their origins because social behavior of this species places a high premium on previous experience by one member of a pair (White and Cade 1971).

Peregrine falcons seem to be nesting on the most common substrates in this portion of the study area. No cliffs occur on the Arctic Coastal Plain or in the transition area between the Coastal Plain and Foothills. Peregrines are essentially ground nesters in these areas, nesting on the tops of sand and mud banks cut by meandering

rivers (Figure 10), beneath willow bushes on the tops or slopes of steep, willow-covered soil and mud banks, or less frequently in abandoned stick nests of rough-legged hawks or on mud banks along lake shorelines. The use of lacustrine habitats for nesting has not previously been recorded for the *tundrius* subspecies in Alaska, and may reflect the use of more marginal habitats close to core habitats in the Coastal Plain–Arctic Foothills transition area. However, a few isolated instances of another North American subspecies (*F. p. anatum*) nesting on cliffs near lakes have been identified in interior Alaska (Mindell 1983). Additionally, ground nesting has been described in parts of Canada (*F. p. tundrius*) and boggy wetlands in Russia (*F. p. calidris*), Fennoscandia, and Europe (*F. p. peregrinus;* Hickey and Anderson 1979).

Many seemingly suitable cliffs in the Arctic Foothills, however, have never been observed to be occupied during surveys in the past 15 years (Appendix A). In the northern portion of this ecoregion, the absence of cliff and bank habitats is obvious, but explanations for low densities of peregrines in the southern Foothills, where cliff structures and improvements such as abandoned stick nests of other

Figure 10. Photographs of (*a*) a typical low, soil bank used by nesting peregrine falcons (*Falco peregrinus tundrius*) on drainages on the Arctic Coastal Plain in the Northeast Planning Unit, National Petroleum Reserve–Alaska; and (*b*) a ground nest site of peregrines at the top of a bluff, upper Price River (center right).

raptors are numerous, are not apparent and are probably related to a number of ecological factors. Peregrine falcons may be avoiding golden eagles (Poole and Bromley 1988). Although peregrines occasionally nest close to golden eagles along interior rivers of Alaska, little overlap is seen with nesting eagles in the NPR–A (Figures 3 and 6). Alternatively, this apparent avoidance of some cliffs may be due to altitudinal limits of peregrines nesting in northern Alaska. Cade (1960) noted that the distribution of peregrine nest sites in Alaska is almost consistently limited by altitude at about 610 m (2,000 feet). A few peregrine nests have been located at higher elevations in northern Alaska (Cade 1960), but such observations are rare. In addition to the presence of eagles and elevation, competition may occur with gyrfalcons or common ravens for nesting substrates or resources, but few data support this hypothesis (White and Cade 1971). Finally, habitat quality (e.g., prey availability) probably differs as one moves inland and may influence peregrine distribution (e.g., increased diversity of wetlands on the Coastal Plain vs. tussock tundra inland).

Gyrfalcons

Adult or young gyrfalcons were located at only 19 sites in 1999, down from 29 in 1977 (Table 8; Ritchie 1979). However, a greater number of sites used by gyrfalcons (41 vs. 29) were documented in 1999 than in 1977 (Table 2). Because of the difference in survey timing noted previously, we cannot be certain whether these observations resulted from population fluctuations or from adult and young birds leaving the nest before our survey was undertaken in 1999. An estimate of the number of gyrfalcon territories in the NPR–A study area would probably range from 30 to 40, excluding those on the main Colville River below its junction with the Etivluk River, where about 40 territories are known (Swem et al. 1994). Both the number of occupied territories and productivity may fluctuate widely in this species (Cade 1960; Shank and Poole 1994), depending on prey availability—especially ptarmigan—and spring weather conditions (Poole 1987). Furthermore, nonbreeding or failed gyrfalcons are not often encountered at nesting territories during brief aerial surveys (Roseneau 1972), complicating an assessment of territory occupancy.

The distribution of gyrfalcon sites in 1999 was similar to that recorded in 1977 (Figure 11), with most sites occurring along drainages in the upper Colville River area (Table 8). As in 1977, gyrfalcons nested on sizable cliffs in the southern Foothills in 1999, and less often on shale bluffs and smaller rock outcrops north of the Colville River.

Golden Eagles

The number of golden eagle nest sites located in the NPR–A was greater in 1999 than in 1977, but in both years less than half of the nests were occupied (Tables 2 and 8). Ten pairs (or incubating adults) were found in 1977 and 11 in 1999. Some of the unoccupied nest locations probably represent golden eagle territories, but their status could not be determined from a single aerial survey. The number of territories probably exceeds our counts of successful nests, however.

The NPR–A is at the northern limit of the breeding range of the golden eagle (Johnson and Herter 1989). In the past, climatic conditions north of the Brooks Range were believed to be too severe for consistent and successful breeding by golden eagles (Hobbie and Cade 1962). But after systematic, multiyear surveys were conducted in the Arctic National Wildlife Refuge in 1988–1990, Young et al. (1995) concluded that golden eagles breed consistently and successfully on the North Slope.

The number of young per successful pair in 1999 (1.2) was similar to results from other studies conducted in arctic areas. In the Arctic National Wildlife Refuge, Young et al. (1995) found 1.1–1.3 young per successful pair from 1988 to 1990; in the Northwest Territories, Poole and Bromley (1988) reported 1.1–1.5 young per successful pair from 1983 to 1986. The number of young per successful pair in the NPR–A in 1977 (1.7) was higher than these, but similar to upper values found in other studies in Alaska south of the Brooks Range (1.3–1.6 young per successful pair, Porcupine River, Ritchie and Curatolo 1982; 1.3–1.7 young per successful pair, Denali National Park, McIntyre 1995). The overall population's productivity (i.e., young per total pairs) and occupancy data for 1999, however, are limited for comparison with other areas because a single, late-season survey results in underestimating total pairs occupying territories.

The distribution of golden eagle nests in 1999 was similar to their distribution in 1977 in

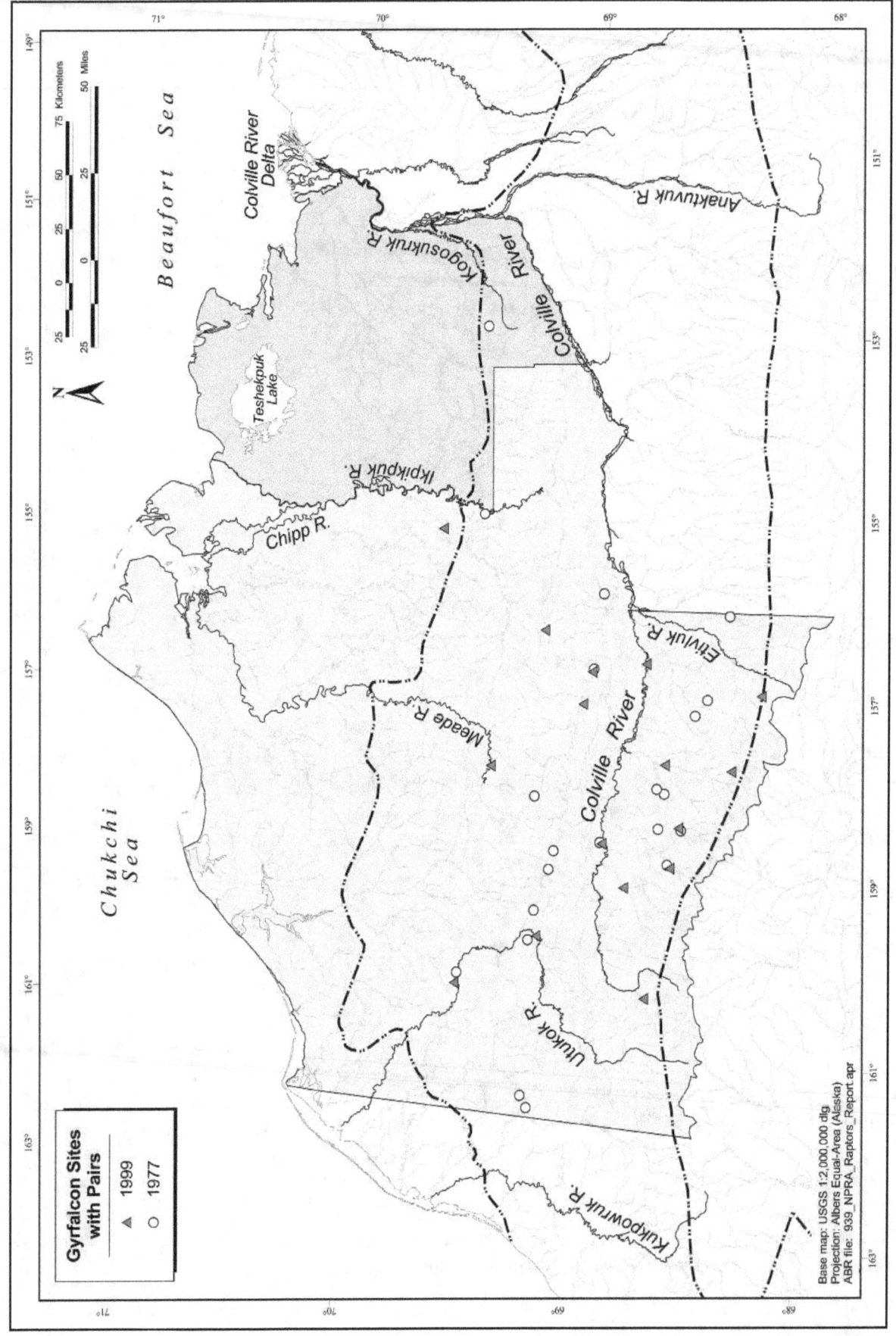

Figure 11. Distribution of gyrfalcon (*Falco rusticolus*) sites with pairs observed during fixed-wing aerial surveys in the National Petroleum Reserve–Alaska, July 1977 and July 1999. Locations are from Ritchie (1977) and the present study. (The dashed lines delineate the three ecoregions: the Arctic Coastal Plain, the Arctic Foothills, and the Brooks Range [see Figure 1].)

Aerial surveys of cliff-nesting raptors in the National Petroleum Reserve–Alaska, 1999, with comparisons to 1977

Table 8. The number of occupied sites (single adults and pairs) of gyrfalcons (*Falco rusticolus*), golden eagles (*Aquila chrysaetos*), and rough-legged hawks (*Buteo lagopus*) in the National Petroleum Reserve–Alaska in 1977 and 1999.

Drainage	Gyrfalcon		Golden Eagle		Rough-legged Hawk	
	1977[a]	1999[b]	1977[a]	1999[b]	1977[a]	1999[b]
Avalik	0	0	0	0	0	1
Awuna	2	2	1	0	5	7
Colville, Upper	2	3	0	2	12	17
Etivluk	1	1	0	0	3	11
Fish Creek	0	0	0	0	1	2
Ikpikpuk	1	0	0	0	0	4
Ipnavik	4	0	2	1	8	13
Ishuktak	NS[c]	0	NS	0	NS	1
Ketik	0	0	0	0	0	0
Kigalik	0	1	0	0	1	5
Kikiakrorak	2	0[d]	0	0[d]	0	5[d]
Kiligwa	3	2	1	2	2	8
Kogosukruk	2	0[d]	0	0[d]	7	21[d]
Kokolik	2	0	1	2	0	2
Kuna	3	2	2	1	8	12
Meade	1	1	0	0	2	4
Nigu	0	0	0	0	3	3
Nuka	0	1	1	0	1	5
Oumalik Lakes	NS	0	NS	0	NS	0
Oumalik River	NS	0	NS	0	NS	0
Titaluk	0	1	0	0	0	2
Topagoruk	NS	0	NS	0	NS	0
Usuktuk	NS	0	NS	0	NS	0
Utukok	6	5	7	4	7	23
Total	29	19	15	12	60	146

[a] Data from 1977 survey by Ritchie (1979).
[b] Data from present survey, except where noted.
[c] NS = indicates that the drainage was not surveyed.
[d] Data from 1997 survey by Swem (1997).

that most nests were found in the southern Foothills (Figure 12). Three active nest sites in 1999 were close to sites that were active in 1977 (Figure 12). Historically and in recent years, subadult (excluding young-of-year) golden eagles have been observed across a wide area of the Arctic Coastal Plain and the northern Foothills region, but nesting has been found only in the southern Foothills region and the Brooks Range (Kessel and Cade 1958; Roseneau 1974; Ritchie 1979; Mauer 1985; Young et al. 1995). The most northerly nests located in the NPR–A during both the 1977 and 1999 surveys were about latitude 69.25°N, and both sites were on the Utukok River or its tributary, Carbon Creek (Ritchie 1977). In the eastern NPR–A, a nest was located on the Colville River at its intersection with Siksikpak Ridge (69.07°N; T. Swem, USFWS, personal communication). In the Arctic National Wildlife Refuge, where the mountains extend farther north than in the NPR–A, occupied golden eagle nest sites occurred between latitudes 69.36° and 69.64°N (Young et al. 1995).

Rough-legged Hawks

In both 1977 and 1999, rough-legged hawks were the most abundant and widespread cliff-nesting raptor in the NPR–A (Table 8). However, twice as many pairs were found in 1999 than in 1977 (Table 2). Nesting densities seemed to be lower in 1977 than in recent years, according to observations made on the lower Colville River (Ritchie 1979). The size and productivity of breeding populations of rough-legged hawks has been shown to vary considerably among years (Kuyt 1980; Poole and Bromley 1988; Swem 1996b). Studies on the lower Colville River between the Etivluk River and Ocean Point showed that the number of pairs occupying territories varied from 53 to 106 (mean=90) over an 11-year period (Swem 1996a).

Because of the difference in timing of the 1977 and 1999 surveys, comparisons of productivity cannot be made. However, the timing of the 1999 survey fell within the period of Swem's (1996a) productivity surveys on the lower Colville River, and the number of young per total pairs found in 1999 (1.9) in the NPR–A was within the range of values (1.6–2.1 young per total pairs) found on the lower Colville River during years when rough-legged hawk numbers were moderate. The overall population's productivity (i.e., young per total pairs) and occupancy data for 1999, however, are limited for comparison with other areas because a single, late-season survey results in underestimating total pairs occupying territories.

The relative distribution of rough-legged hawks in the NPR–A was similar in 1977 and 1999 (Table 2, Figure 13). About 75% of the pairs nested in the southern Foothills south of the Colville River in both years. Most nests were on shale bluffs, riverine cliffs, or scree slopes, which are common substrates along the braided streams of the southern Foothills. Few nests were found on the Arctic Coastal Plain (Figure 13).

Nest Site Habitat Assessment

Surveys conducted in 1999 identified many sand and mud banks north of the Arctic Foothills in a transition area between the Foothills and Coastal Plain. These habitats were considered marginal for raptors, including peregrine falcons, in the 1970s because so few birds had been recorded there. However, results of our 1999 survey suggest that earlier appraisals were inaccurate and that fair-to-good habitat does extend into the Coastal Plain at elevations under 100 m and

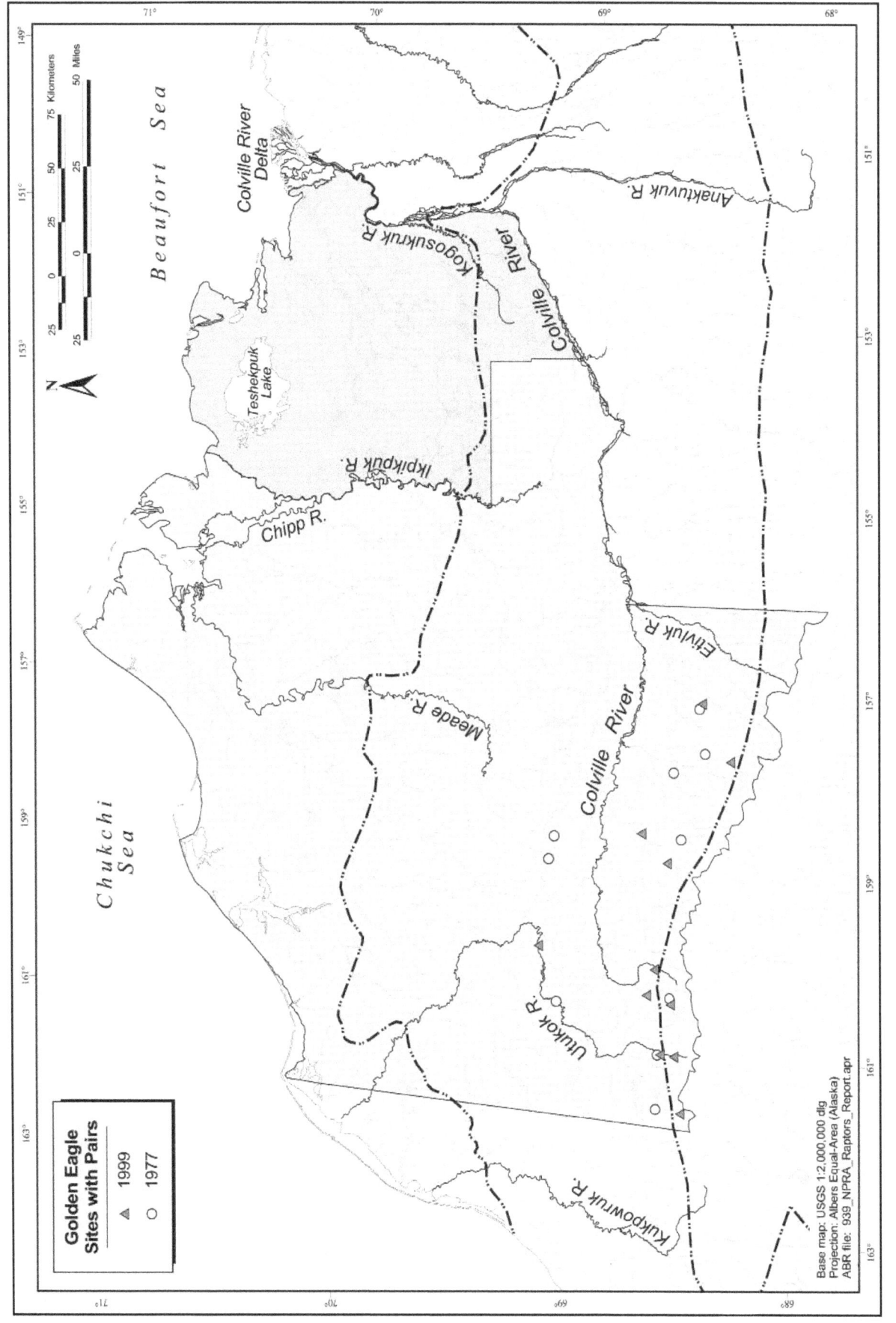

Figure 12. Distribution of golden eagle (*Aquila chrysaetos*) sites with pairs observed during fixed-wing aerial surveys in the National Petroleum Reserve–Alaska, July 1977 and July 1999. Locations are from Ritchie (1977) and the present study. (The dashed lines delineate the three ecoregions: the Arctic Coastal Plain, the Arctic Foothills, and the Brooks Range [see Figure 1].)

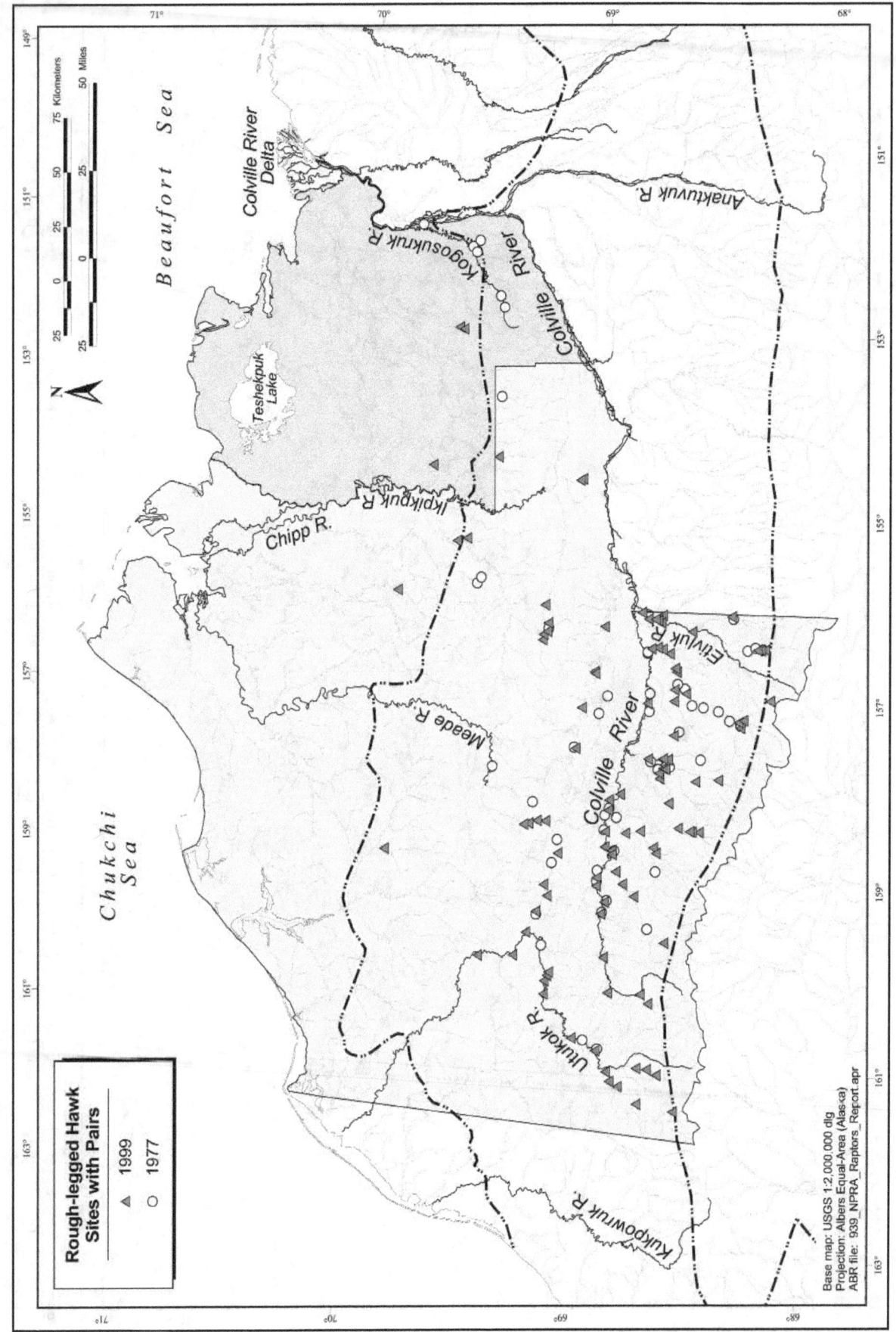

Figure 13. Distribution of rough-legged hawk (*Buteo lagopus*) sites with pairs observed during fixed-wing aerial surveys in the National Petroleum Reserve–Alaska, July 1977 and July 1999. Locations are from Ritchie (1977) and the present study. (The dashed lines delineate the three ecoregions: the Arctic Coastal Plain, the Arctic Foothills, and the Brooks Range [see Figure 1].)

south of about 70°N latitude. Waterfowl surveys north of about 70°N latitude between the Meade and Colville Rivers have not encountered nesting peregrines (R. Ritchie, unpublished notes) in this portion of the Coastal Plain, but occasional bluffs associated with lakes and rivers might attract peregrine falcons for nesting. In addition, some riverine and lacustrine areas west of the Meade River may have occasional banks suitable for nesting. This area requires better survey coverage. A nest was recorded in this region on the Kaolak River (R. King, USFWS, personal communication) and peregrines have been observed at Dewline Sites and on steep coastal mud banks west of Barrow. Peregrines have also been found nesting in coastal areas in northwestern Alaska and near Kaktovik on the Arctic Coast (F. Mauer, USFWS, personal communication). These observations suggest nesting may occur even farther north than 70°N latitude. With a recovered and perhaps still expanding peregrine falcon population in northern Alaska, it would not be prudent to conclude the absence of these falcons in any northern areas until demonstrated by more intensive surveys.

Survey Efficacy Recommendations

The quality of data collected from fixed-wing aircraft for raptors, particularly falcons, can be influenced greatly by the complexity of nesting substrates, experience of the observer, and the timing of the surveys. In regard to timing, questions arise about the comparability of our aerial surveys conducted during different phases of the breeding season. For instance, surveys in 1977 coincided with the incubation through early nestling stage of peregrine falcons, whereas surveys in 1999 were conducted during the midnestling period for this species. What effect this difference in survey timing has on comparable results probably varies by species, but it influences most the comparison of occupancy for all species. That is, given the later surveys in 1999, occupancy estimates may have been lower for each species because failed and nonbreeding pairs would be absent or less conspicuous on their territories later in the season.

In 1977, our surveys occurred at a time when peregrine falcon adults sit more tightly (i.e., late in the incubation through early nestling period) and may not be

as conspicuous from an aircraft platform as they are later in the year. Most incubating adults should have been detected, however, because small cliffs typical of the region can be thoroughly searched by fixed-wing aircraft. Cade and White (1976) searched much of the southern Foothills in 1975 and were convinced that only the occasional pair occurred in the area even if they had missed half of the incubating peregrines. Numbers of peregrine falcons were lowest during the mid-1970s in their core breeding areas in northern Alaska (Colville and Sagavanirktok Rivers; Ambrose et al. 1988), and aerial survey results in this period support a general consensus that peregrine falcons were even more greatly reduced in tributaries and smaller drainages in northern Alaska than along the main rivers (Cade and White 1976).

In 1999, in an effort to get the most information on relative distribution, abundance, and productivity, we conducted our surveys during a period when young peregrines were more obvious and adults were regularly defensive of their young (i.e., midnestling period). As mentioned previously, we probably missed some failed or nonbreeding pairs of peregrine falcons at this time, which may have been absent or inconspicuous during our visit. Despite this limitation, conducting this survey was a cost-effective way to verify the extent of recovery of peregrine falcons in the region and to create a map of the present distribution and relative abundance of peregrines, as well as other raptors, in the NPR–A.

We recommend at least three changes in procedure to improve the value of future fixed-wing aircraft raptor surveys in the region. First, two surveys—one during incubation and a second during the nestling stage—would improve the accuracy of calculations of occupancy and productivity (Steenof 1987). Second, "truthing" fixed-wing coverage with helicopter or ground techniques would provide a means for more accurately obtaining a census of the population and would provide a better baseline for continued population monitoring. Finally, with increased oil exploration interest on the Arctic Coastal Plain, lakeshore nesting habitats for peregrine falcons, such as those identified in the Oumalik Lakes area, should be identified and mapped. Beyond improving our understanding of the recovery of peregrines in the region, identification of these habitats would be important for planning activities outside floodplain cliffs and banks normally considered primary raptor habitats.

Acknowledgments

This project was funded by the Bureau of Land Management (BLM). Additional logistics support was provided by the Fairbanks and Anaktuvuk Pass offices of the National Park Service (NPS) and the Ivotuk field camp of the Polar Ice Coring Group (PICO). We thank Scott Hillard, Camp Manager for PICO at Ivotuk, and Mike Haubert and Shelly Swanson (NPS) for their help in the field. Peter Bente (Alaska Department of Fish and Game) and Ted Swem (U.S. Fish and Wildlife Service) provided records from their survey work on the Utukok and Colville Rivers, respectively. Both Peter and Ted, in addition to Tim Craig (BLM), provided critical reviews of earlier drafts of this report. Mike Kunz (BLM) generously opened his field camp at Inigok to offer rest and a break from flying. Devonee Harshburger, Will Lentz, Alice Stickney, and Allison Zusi-Cobb from ABR, Inc., provided graphic, editorial, and word processing assistance for the final report, which preceded this technical report. Sandy Hamilton, Arctic Air Alaska, provided his companionship, good humor, and incredible skill at piloting his aircraft. His expertise greatly contributed to the success of this program.

Photo courtesy of the Bureau of Land Management.

Literature Cited

Ambrose, R. E., R. J. Ritchie, C. M. White, P. F. Schempf, T. Swem, and R. Dittrick. 1988. Changes in the status of peregrine falcon populations in Alaska. Pages 73–82 *in* T. J. Cade, J. H. Enderson, C. G. Thelander, and C. M. White (editors). Peregrine falcon populations, their management, and recovery. The Peregrine Fund, Boise, Idaho.

Cade, T. J. 1960. Ecology of the peregrine and gyrfalcon populations in Alaska. University of California Publications in Zoology 63:51–290.

Cade, T. J., and C. M. White. 1976. Colville River watershed. Pages 245–48 *in* R. W. Fyfe, S. A. Temple, and T. J. Cade (editors). The 1975 North American peregrine falcon survey. Canadian Field-Naturalist 90:228–273.

Fyfe, R., and R. Olendorff. 1976. Minimizing the dangers of nesting studies to raptors and other sensitive species. Canadian Wildlife Service, Occasional Paper 23. 17 pp.

Gallant, A. L., E. F. Binnian, J. M. Omernik, and M. B. Shasby. 1996. Ecoregions of Alaska. U.S. Geological Survey Professional Paper 1567, Washington, D.C. 73 pp.

Hickey, J. J., and D. W. Anderson. 1979. The peregrine falcon: Life history and population literature. Pages 3–42 *in* J. J. Hickey, editor, Peregrine falcon populations, University of Wisconsin Press, Madison.

Hobbie, J. E., and T. J. Cade. 1962. Observations on the breeding of golden eagles at Lake Peters in northern Alaska. Condor 64:235–237.

Johnson, S. R., and D. R. Herter. 1989. Birds of the Beaufort Sea. BP Exploration, Anchorage, Alaska. 372 pp.

Kessel, B., and T. J. Cade. 1958. Birds of the Colville River, northern Alaska. University of Alaska, Biological Paper 2. 83 pp.

King, R. 1979. Results of aerial surveys of migratory birds on NPR–A in 1977 and 1978. Pages 187–226 *in* P. C. Lent (editor). Studies of selected wildlife and fish and their use of habitats on and adjacent to NPR–A, 1977–1978. Vol. 1. NPR–A Work Group 3, Anchorage, Alaska.

Kuyt, E. 1980. Distribution and breeding of raptors in the Thelon River area, Northwest Territories, 1957–1969. Canadian Field-Naturalist 94:121–130.

Mauer, F. J. 1985. Distribution and relative abundance of golden eagles in relation to the Porcupine caribou herd during calving and post-calving periods, 1984. Pages 114–144 *in* G. W. Garner and P. E. Reynolds (editors). 1984 update report of baseline studies of fish, wildlife, and their habitats. U.S. Fish and Wildlife Service, Anchorage, Alaska.

McGowan, J. 1973. Raptor survey-inventory progress report—1971. Pages 140–143 *in* D. E. McKnight, editor. Alaska Department of. Fish and Game, Federal Aid in Wildlife Restoration, Survey-Inventory Management Report, Part III: Small game and raptors, Project W-17-4, Juneau, Alaska.

McIntyre, C. L. 1995. Nesting ecology of migratory golden eagles (*Aquila chrysaetos*) in Denali National Park, Alaska. M.S. Thesis, University of Alaska, Fairbanks. 57 pp.

Mindell, D. P. 1983. Nesting raptors in southwestern Alaska: Status, distribution, and aspects of biology. U.S. Bureau of Land Management, Alaska Technical Report 8. 59 pp.

Poole, K. G. 1987. Aspects of the ecology, food habits, and foraging characteristics of gyrfalcons in the central Canadian arctic. M.S. Thesis, University of Alberta, Edmonton. 65 pp.

Poole, K. G., and R. G. Bromley. 1988. Interrelationships within a raptor guild in the central Canadian Arctic. Canadian Journal of Zoology 66:2275–2282.

Ritchie, R. J. 1977. Inventory and evaluation of, and recommendations for, cliff-nesting raptor habitat in Naval Petroleum Reserve–Alaska (NPR–A). U.S. Fish and Wildlife Service, Anchorage, Alaska. 88 pp.

Ritchie, R. J. 1979. A survey of cliff-nesting raptors and their habitats. Pages 313–36 *in* P. C. Lent (editor). Studies of selected wildlife and fish and their use of habitats on and adjacent to NPR–A, 1977–1978. Vol. 2. NPR–A Work Group 3, Anchorage, Alaska.

Ritchie, R. J., and J. A. Curatolo. 1982. Notes on golden eagle productivity and nest site characteristics, Porcupine River, Alaska, 1979–1982. Raptor Research 16:23–127.

Roseneau, D. G. 1972. The summer distribution and food habits of the gyrfalcon (*Falco rusticolus*) on the Seward Peninsula, Alaska. M.S. Thesis, University of Alaska, Fairbanks. 124 pp.

Roseneau, D. G. 1974. A continuation of studies of raptorial bird nesting sites along proposed pipeline routes in Alaska. Final report prepared for Northern Engineering Services Company, Ltd., and Canadian Arctic Gas Study Company, Ltd., Calgary, Alberta, by Renewable Resources Consulting Services Ltd. 69 pp. + photos

Shank, C. C., and K. G. Poole. 1994. Status of gyrfalcon (*Falco rusticolus*) populations in the Northwest Territories, Canada. Pages 421–436 *in* B. U. Meyburg and R. D. Chancellor (editors). Raptor Conservation Today: Proceedings of the IV World Conference on Birds of Prey and Owls, Berlin, Germany.

Silva, J. B. 1985b. The 1983 peregrine falcon/raptor survey along the Utukok and Sagavanirktok Rivers. Open File Report 11. U.S. Department of the Interior, Bureau of Land Management, Fairbanks, Alaska. 19 pp.

Steenof, K. 1987. Assessing raptor reproductive success and productivity. Pages 157–170 *in* B. A. Giron Pendleton, B. A. Millsap, K. W. Cline, and D. M. Bird (editors). Raptor management techniques manual. National Wildlife Federation, Washington, D.C.

Swem, T. R. 1996b. Aspects of the breeding biology of rough-legged hawks along the Colville River, Alaska. M.S. Thesis, Boise State University, Idaho. 78 pp.

Swem, T., C. McIntyre, R. J. Ritchie, P. J. Bente, and D. G. Roseneau. 1994. Distribution, abundance, and notes on the breeding biology of gyrfalcons (*Falco rusticolus*) in Alaska. Pages 437–446 *in* B. Meyburg and R. Chancellor (editors). Raptor Conservation Today: Proceedings of the IV World Conference on Birds of Prey and Owls. Helm Information Ltd., East Sussex, England. 799 pp.

White, C. M., and D. A. Boyce. 1978. A profile of various rivers and their raptor populations in western Alaska, 1977. Final report prepared for U.S. Department of the Interior, Bureau of Land Management, Anchorage, Alaska. 77 pp.

White, C. M., and T. J. Cade. 1971. Cliff-nesting raptors and ravens along the Colville River, Arctic Alaska. Living Bird 10:107–150.

White, C. M., and T. J. Cade. 1975. Raptor studies along the proposed Susitna powerline corridors, oil pipeline, and in the Yukon and Colville River regions of Alaska. Final report prepared for U.S. Fish and Wildlife Service, Bureau of Land Management, National Park Service, Arctic Institute of North America, and American Museum of Natural History. 28 pp.

Wright, J. W., and P. J. Bente. 1999. Documentation of active peregrine falcon nest sites. ADFG, Division of Wildlife Conservation, Federal Aid in Wildlife Restoration, Final Research Report. Grants SE-2-9, 10, 11. 15 pp.

Young, D. D., C. L. McIntyre, P. J. Bente, T. R. McCabe, and R. E. Ambrose. 1995. Nesting by golden eagles on the North Slope of the Brooks Range in northeastern Alaska. Journal of Field Ornithology 66:373–79.

Unpublished References

Bente, P. J. 1989. Northwest Alaska raptor survey. Unpublished survey summary. U.S. Fish and Wildlife Service, Endangered Species, Fairbanks, Alaska. 2 pp.

Cade, T. J., J. R. Haugh, and C. M. White. 1971. Ecology and current status of cliff-nesting raptors in Arctic Alaska. Unpublished survey summary prepared for the National Science Foundation, Tundra Biome Program. 22 pp.

Dittrick, R. 1990. Raptor observations on the Utukok River, 1990. Raptor observation record card and map. 1 pp.

Dittrick, R., and L. Moorehead. 1983. Productivity and status of cliff nesting raptors along the Colville River and selected tributaries, Alaska, 1983. Unpublished report prepared for the U.S. Fish and Wildlife Service, Office of Endangered Species, Anchorage, Alaska, by Biological Investigative Research Services. 37 pp.

Dittrick, R., and T. Swem. 1981. Productivity and status of cliff nesting raptors along the Colville River and selected areas within the National Petroleum Reserve–Alaska. Unpublished report prepared for U.S. Fish and Wildlife Service, Office of Endangered Species, Anchorage, Alaska, by Biological Investigative Research Services. 45 pp.

Hunter, R. E 1984. Colville River raptor survey, 1984. Unpublished field notes. U.S. Fish and Wildlife Service, Anchorage, Alaska. 19 pp.

Karlen, R. R., and R. L. Masinton. 1991. The 1991 peregrine falcon/raptor survey, Kiligwa and Etivluk Rivers, Alaska. Unpublished report. U.S. Department of the Interior, Bureau of Land Management, Arctic District Office, Fairbanks, Alaska. 12 pp.

King, R. 1978. Kogosukruk River raptor survey, July 20–27, 1978. Unpublished memorandum. U.S. Fish and Wildlife Service, Fairbanks, Alaska. 3 pp. + map

Pegau, R. E. 1975. Raptor nesting in the western Brooks Range. Letter of 13 June *to* R. A. Hinman, State of Alaska, Division of Game, *from* R. E. Pegau, State of Alaska, Division of Game, Nome. 3 pp.

Ritchie, R. J. 1986. Raptor surveys of the Ikpikpuk, Nanushuk-Anaktuvuk, Toolik, Ivishak, Canning, and Jago Rivers, 1986. Letter of 26 August *to* R. E. Ambrose, U.S. Fish and Wildlife Service, Fairbanks, Alaska, *from* R. J. Ritchie, Alaska Biological Research, Inc., Fairbanks, Alaska. 6 pp.

Ritchie, R. J. 1988. Peregrine falcon survey of the Central Brooks Range, 1988. Unpublished survey map. Alaska Biological Research, Inc., Fairbanks, Alaska. 1 p. [map]

Ritchie, R. J. 1989. Peregrine falcon survey of the Central Brooks Range, 1989. Letter of 20 November *to* R. E. Ambrose, U.S. Fish and Wildlife Service, Fairbanks, Alaska, *from* R. J. Ritchie, Alaska Biological Research, Inc., Fairbanks, Alaska. 4 pp.

Ritchie, R. J. 1992. Peregrine falcon survey of the Central Brooks Range, 1992. Letter of 13 August *to* T. Swem, U.S. Fish and Wildlife Service, Fairbanks, Alaska, *from* R. J. Ritchie, Alaska Biological Research, Inc., Fairbanks, Alaska. 14 pp.

Silva, J. 1984. 1984 peregrine falcon/raptor survey, preliminary status report. Unpublished report. U.S. Department of. Interior, Bureau of Land Management, Fairbanks, Alaska. 2 pp. + maps

Silva, J. B. 1985a. The 1985 peregrine falcon/raptor survey, preliminary status report. Unpublished report. U.S. Department of the Interior, Bureau of Land Management, Fairbanks, Alaska. 2 pp. + maps

Silva, J. B., and R. L. Masinton. 1986. The 1986 peregrine falcon/raptor survey along the Colville (Ipnavik River to Ocean Point) and Sagavanirktok Rivers, including portions of the Killik, Etivluk, and Kogosukruk Rivers. Unpublished report. U.S. Department of the Interior, Bureau of Land Management, Fairbanks, Alaska. 29 pp.

Silva, J. B., and R. L. Masinton. 1987. The 1987 peregrine falcon/raptor survey along the Colville, Utukok, and Sagavanirktok Rivers, including selected tributaries. Unpublished report. U.S. Department of the Interior, Bureau of Land Management, Fairbanks, Alaska. 28 pp.

Silva, J. B., and R. L. Masinton. 1988. The 1988 peregrine falcon/raptor survey, Central Arctic Alaska. Unpublished report. U.S. Department of the Interior, Bureau of Land Management, Fairbanks, Alaska. 23 pp.

Silva, J. B., and R. L. Masinton. 1990. The 1990 peregrine falcon/raptor survey, Ipnavik River, Alaska. Unpublished report. U.S. Department of. Interior, Bureau of Land Management, Fairbanks, Alaska. 11 pp.

Swem, T. R. 1985. The 1985 Colville River raptor survey. Unpublished report. U.S. Department of. Interior, Bureau of Land Management, Fairbanks, Alaska. 22 pp. + appendixes

Swem, T. R. 1987. The 1987 Colville River raptor survey. Unpublished report. U.S. Department of the Interior, Bureau of Land Management, Fairbanks, Alaska. 19 pp.

Swem, T. R. 1988. The 1988 Colville River raptor survey. Unpublished report. U.S. Department of the Interior, Bureau of Land Management, Fairbanks, Alaska. 17 pp.

Swem, T. R. 1989. 1989 Colville River raptor survey. Unpublished survey summary. U.S. Fish and Wildlife Service, Fairbanks, Alaska. 4 pp.

Swem, T. R. 1990. 1990 Colville River raptor survey. Unpublished survey summary. U.S. Fish and Wildlife Service, Fairbanks, Alaska. 4 pp.

Swem, T. R. 1991. 1991 Colville River raptor survey. Unpublished survey summary. U.S. Fish and Wildlife Service, Fairbanks, Alaska. 5 pp.

Swem, T. R. 1992. 1992 Colville River raptor survey. Unpublished survey summary. U.S. Fish and Wildlife Service, Fairbanks, Alaska. 5 pp.

Swem, T. R. 1993. 1993 Colville River raptor survey. Unpublished report. U.S. Fish and Wildlife Service, Fairbanks, Alaska. 8 pp.

Swem, T. R. 1994. 1994 Colville River raptor survey. Unpublished report. U.S. Fish and Wildlife Service, Fairbanks, Alaska. 8 pp.

Swem, T. R. 1995. 1995 Colville River raptor survey. Unpublished report. U.S. Fish and Wildlife Service, Fairbanks, Alaska. 10 pp.

Swem, T. R. 1996a. 1996 Colville River raptor survey. Unpublished report. U.S. Fish and Wildlife Service, Fairbanks, Alaska. 10 pp.

Swem, T. R. 1997. 1997 Colville River raptor survey. Unpublished report. U.S. Fish and Wildlife Service, Fairbanks, AK. 13 pp.

Swem, T. R., B. Dittrick, and J. Silva. 1982. The 1982 peregrine falcon/raptor survey in Central Arctic Alaska. Unpublished report. U.S. Department of the Interior, Bureau of Land Management, Fairbanks, Alaska. 30 pp. + maps

Todd, C. T. 1978. Surveillance of the Colville River, 1978. Unpublished report. U.S. Fish and Wildlife Service, Fairbanks, Alaska. 17 pp.

Watts, A. B. 1995. Raptor observations on the Colville, Kurupa, Etivluk, Chandler, Anaktuvuk Rivers, and September and Prince Creeks, 1995. Letter of 17 October *to* T. Swem, U.S. Fish and Wildlife Service, Fairbanks, Alaska, *from* A. B. Watts, ARCO Alaska, Inc., Anchorage. 3 pp.

Watts, A. B. 1997. Raptor observations on the Colville, Kiligwa, Kukpowruk, Utukok Rivers, 1997. Letter of 12 March *to* T. Swem, U.S. Fish and Wildlife Service, Fairbanks, Alaska, *from* A. B. Watts, ARCO Alaska, Inc., Anchorage. 1 p.

Appendix A

The number of sites occupied by peregrine falcons (*Falco peregrinus tundrius*) in the National Petroleum Reserve–Alaska, 1952–1999.

Numbers in bold text indicate years when complete surveys of drainages were conducted. Numbers in regular text indicate years when partial surveys of drainages were conducted or when incidental observations of peregrine falcons at territories were reported. A zero indicates that a survey was conducted, but no peregrine falcons were found occupying a territory. Surveys included aircraft, ground, and boat techniques. Data for complete surveys of the Lower Colville River are from Swem (unpublished data); other source information is noted.

Drainage	1952	1959	1967	1968	1969	1971	1973	1975	1977	1978	1979	1980	1981	1982
Avalik									0					
Awuna								0	0					
Colville - Lower	32	35	27	32	33	25	14		3	15	16	21	24	26
Colville - Upper	8					0		3	1					2
Etivluk								2	2	1			1	2
Fish Creek									0					
Ikpikpuk									0					
Ipnavik								0	0					0
Ishuktak														
Ketik								0	0					
Kigalik									0				0	
Kikiakrorak									0	1				1
Kiligwa								0	0					
Kogosukruk									1	2			4	3
Kokolik								0	1					
Kuna								0	1					
Meade								0	0				0	
Nigu								0	0					
Nuka								0	0					
Oumalik Lake														
Oumalik River														
Titaluk									0					
Topagoruk														
Usuktuk														
Utukok						1		0	0					0
Total	40	35	27	32	33	26	14	5	9	19	16	21	29	34
Sources	a					b		c	d	e			f	g

a	Cade and White 1976	h	Dittrick and Moorehead 1983, Silva 1985b
b	Cade et al. 1971, McGowan 1973	i	Hunter 1984, Silva 1984
c	Pegau 1975, White and Cade 1975	j	Silva 1985a, Swem 1985
d	White and Boyce 1978, Ritchie 1979	k	Ritchie 1986, Silva and Masinton 1986
e	King 1978, Todd 1978	l	Silva and Masinton 1987, Swem 1987
f	Dittrick and Swem 1981	m	Ritchie 1988, Silva and Masinton 1988, Swem 1988
g	Swem et al. 1982		

	1983	1984	1985	1986	1987	1988	1989	1990	1991	1992	1993	1994	1995	1996	1997	1998	1999
																	2
					0										1		0
	26	**31**	**29**	**33**	**36**	**46**	**53**	**50**	**55**	**56**	**58**	**61**	**56**	**57**	**57**	**62**	**56**
		0	1		3	1	4	1	2	1	1	1	1		2		9
	2	1	1	0	3	2			1	1			1				2
																	9
				2		2				6							15
					1	1		2									2
																	2
																	0
																	1
		1			1	1	2						2	1	7		3
					1	0			0								3
	2	2	3	2	3	3	9	1	1	1	3	2	2	4	**21**		2
					1		1										1
					2	1											0
																	0
	0		**0**		**1**	0											0
																	4
																	1
										1							5
																	4
																	2
	0		**0**		**2**		**2**	1						1			**13**
	30	35	34	37	54	57	71	55	59	66	62	64	62	65	87	62	133
	h	i	j	k	l	m	n	o	p	q	r	s	t	u	v		w

n   Bente 1989, Ritchie 1989, Swem 1989

o   Dittrick 1990, Silva and Masinton 1990, Swem 1990

p   Karlen and Masinton 1991, Swem 1991

q   Ritchie 1992, Swem 1992

r   Swem 1993

s   Swem 1994

t   Swem 1995, Watts 1995

u   Swem 1996a, Watts 1997

v   Swem 1997, Kunz 1998 (maps)

w   Present study, Bente (unpublished notes) and Swem (unpublished data)

Appendix B

Height (in meters) is referred to by numeric height classes.[a] Area numbers are keyed to the map (Appendix Figure B.1) following this table (Ritchie 1979); photo samples (Appendix Figure B.2) of these substrate types follow the map.

Drainage or Area	Substrate Types[b] and Occurrence
1. Anuk Creek	South-facing 2-3 SB along lower 10 km; 1-3 RC–O in upper reaches
2. Archimedes and Lookout Ridges	3 EF fractured rock near tops of these ridges
3. Avalik River	3 MB at boundary of northern foothills extending into coastal plains
4. Avingak Creek	Not extensively surveyed but probably limited, small O–ST
5. Awuna River	3 SB and 2-3 RC along 270 km of river; large RC at lat 69°06', long 156°43'
6. Brooks Range (Central)	Fairly gentle topography between the upper Kuna and Nigu; 1-2 ST slopes
7. Brooks Range (De Long Mtns)	West of Kuna there are more 1-3 RC–O than Central portion, but restricted
8. Carbon Creek	South-facing 2-3 SB–EF nearly entire 60 km of river
9. Colville River (upper Kiligwa River	Scattered 2-3 SB, some 1-2 RC, downriver from the mouth of the Nuka River
10. Colville River (between Kiligwa and Etivluk Rivers)	Widely scattered 3 SB and ST
11. Colville River (Etivluk River to Ocean Pt.)	2-3 SB, RC above Umiat; 1-3 MB with RC below Umiat described in White and Cade (1971)
12. Cula Creek	Few O–SB in upper Cula
13. Cutaway Creek	Scattered 2-3 RC and smaller O in upper portion
14. Driftwood Creek	A few 3 SB along the river
15. East Fork Etivluk River	Scattered east-facing 3 SB in upper portion
16. Ekakevik Mountain	Approximately 30 km^2 with scattered 2-3, O–RC
17. Etivluk River uplands and western edge of Ivotuk Hills	Rolling tundra with occasional O

Drainage or Area	Substrate Types[b] and Occurrence
18. Grayling Creek	A few 3 SB; a single 2 SB–RC near confluence with Colville 30km
19. Ikpikpuk River	Scattered 3 MB–SB in upper portions; rock exposure on bank at Little Supreme Bluff (lat 69°36', long 154°57'); lower soil banks and sand dunes increase beneath this point
20. Ipnavik River (lower)	Similar to main Etivluk; numerous and widely spaced 3 SB
21. Ipnavik River (mid-upper)	ST in upper reaches; numerous 2 RC–SB (with at least three 1 RC between Memorial Creek and north of Crassico Creek); Memorial, Bupto, Ekakevik and Taffy Creeks have 1-2 RC
22. Iteriak Creek	Approximately 5 km of west-facing 3 SB
23. Iteriak Ridge	Approximately 5 km of O
24. Judy, Wolf, Alice, and Fry Creeks lat 69°30' and 69°45'	3 MB common up to 25 m in height as creeks leave foothills; most common between
25. Kaksu River (tributary of Meade)	upper 20 km scattered EF and 2-3 RC
26. Ketik River	3 EF in headwaters; 3 MB where river enters coastal plains
27. Kigalik River	Lower 90 km has only a few SB–ST less than 15 m in height; however, a small canyon 12 km in length near VABM 937 (Kigal) includes 2 RC, SB, and EF
28. Kikiakrorak River	Numerous 2-3 MB, with 3 RC in headwaters of main Kikiakrorak; MB not as high as those on Kogosukruk (generally less than 25 m)
29. Kiligwa River (lower)	Scattered 3 SB
30. Kiligwa River (upper) Rolling	Canyon between Rolling Pin Creek and Strident Creek providing 1-2 RC; above Pin Creek more ST and fewer RC; RC on Jubilee, Rolling Pin, and Panic Creeks
31. Knifeblade, Kimipak, and other ridges north of Colville but east of the Ikpikpuk	Occasional 3 O–EF, mostly rolling tundra
32. Kogosukruk River	Numerous 2-3 MB, some with limited rock outcropping; rock increases as headwaters are approached; 3 RC in west fork headwaters of his river
33. Kokolik River	Numerous 2 RC and EF above Avingak Creek and extending outside boundary of NPR-A; below Avingak Creek three 3 RC–ST with ledges

Drainage or Area	Substrate Types[b] and Occurrence
34. Kulugra, Shaningarok, and other ridges north of Colville, but west of Ikpikpuk	No O or EF; rolling tundra
35. Kuna River	Lower section a broad valley with scattered 2-3 SB, with occasional O north of Monument Ridge. Upper Kuna has few RC, similar to upper Ipnavik, with ST prevailing
36. Kutchaurak Creek	Few scattered 3 SB–RC
37. Liberator Ridge-Swayback Mountain-Cockscomb Ridge	Numerous but scattered 1-2 RC–O
38. Lily Creek (tributary of Meade)	Upper 10 km has scattered EF and 2-3 RC
39. Lisburne Ridge	2-3 O, amidst steep ST slopes
40. Lookout River	Two main stretches, each approximately 2 km long, of 2 SB on north side of river; slumping 3 MB in headwaters; occasional SB near confluence with Awuna
41. Lost Temper Creek	Approximately 5 km of 2-3 SB along upper portion
42. Main Etivluk River	Numerous 2-3 SB with occasional RC on lower Etivluk; ST in the Howard Pass area; small 2-4 km canyons with 2 RC on Fay and Tukuto Creeks
43. Main Utukok River	Lower river between lat 69°45' and Eskimo Hill has at least five 3 RC and ST; above Carbon Creek and below Driftwood 2-3 RC and EF in two major canyons; 2-3 SB between these canyons
44. Maybe Creek and tributaries	3 MB with some rock exposure; single 3 RC and 1-km stretch of SB near head of September Creek
45. Meade River	2-3 MB and ST along river at northern edge of foothills; few 3 RC on upper Meade; single 2 RC at lat 69°32', long 157°52'
46. Mesas from Meat Mountain to the Kiligwa River	3 EF of highly fractured rock; rolling tundra
47. Monument Ridge-Rim Butte-Mt. Bupto	Scattered 1-3 RC–O with some areas of ST
48. Nigu River	A few RC and SB such as Nigu Bluff in foothills section; ST in mountains with a few rock exposures

Drainage or Area	Substrate Types[b] and Occurrence
49. Nuka River (lower)	Occasional 3 SB
50. Nuka River (upper)	Above Pilly Fork, scattered 1-3 RC and O in constricted valley, similar terrain in Mechanic and Sorepaw Creeks
51. Otuk Creek	2 SB; large isolated RC lat 68°39', long 155°45'
52. Prince Creek	Numerous north-facing 3 MB
53. Puvakrat Mountain	A few 2-3 O
54. Shaningarok Creek	No exposures along creek; limited rock exposure along ridgelines in headwaters
55. Smith Mountain	Rolling tundra with some ST, no RC
56. Swayback Creek	5-km stretch of 1-2 RC near confluence with Kuna
57. Titaluk River	Upper River featureless; area approximately 35 km upriver from confluence with Ikpikpuk contains 2 MB (50 m); lower Bronx Creek similar
58. Tributaries on north side of Awuna	Lower sections of these creeks (about 20 km) contain a few scattered 3 SB, EF, and RC less than 15 m

[a]Height classes:

1 = more than 100 m (330 feet)

2 = 50 to 100 m (165 to 330 feet)

3 = less than 50 m (165 feet)

[b]Substrate types:

Shalebanks = SB

Mud or sand banks = MB

Scree and Talus slopes = ST

Rock cliffs = RC

Escarpment faces = EF

Outcrops = O

Appendix Figure B.1. Distribution of habitat classes for cliff-nesting raptors (Ritchie 1979).

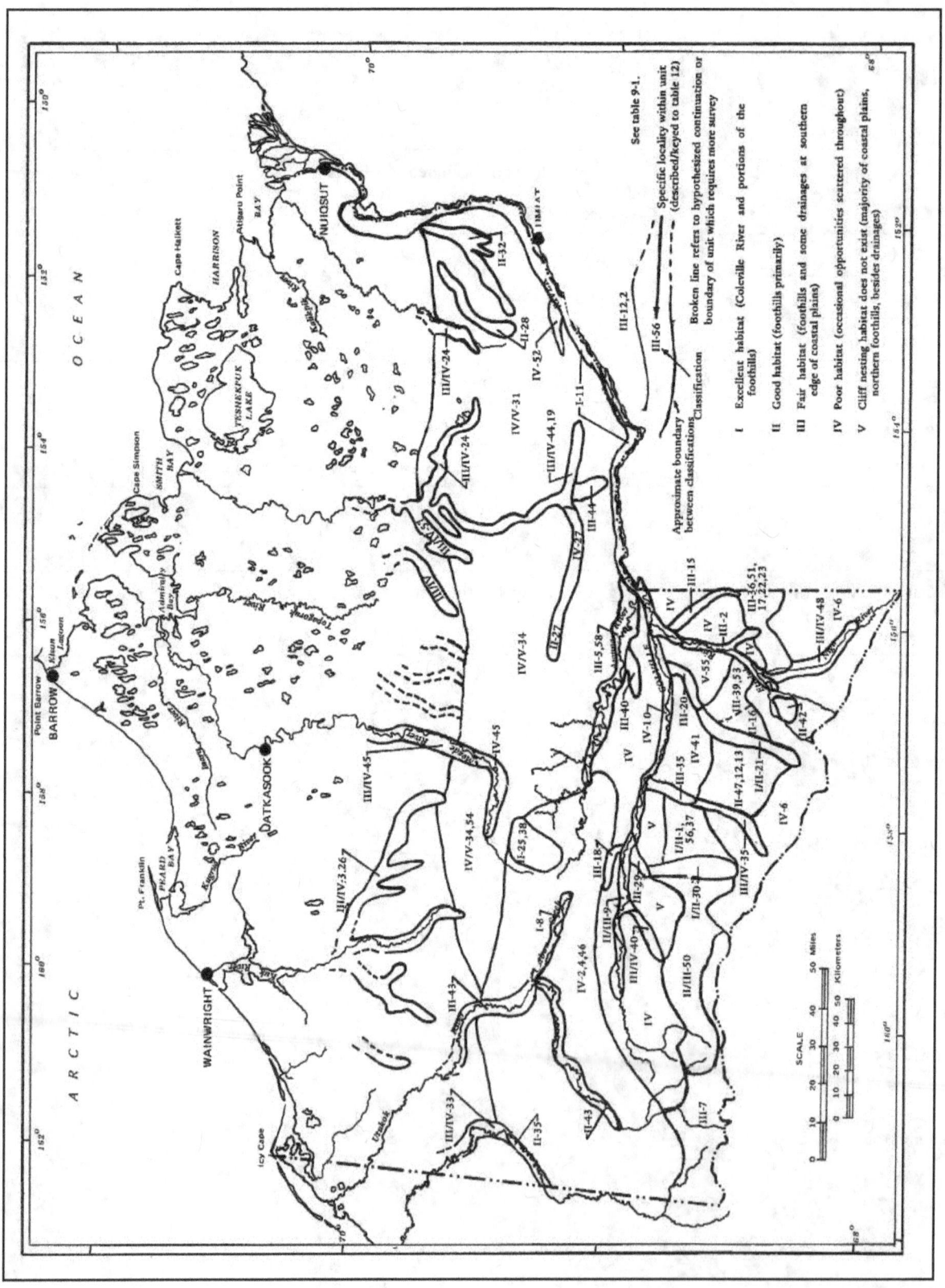

Appendix Figure B.2. Habitat types, National Petroleum Reserve–Alaska.

(a) Escarpment face (EF) on upper Kokolik River.

(b) Shale banks (SB) on Ipnavik River.

(c) Soil and mud banks (MB) on lower Titaluk River.

(d) Minaret outcrops (O) on Lisburne Ridge.

(e) Rock cliffs (RC) along the Kiligwa River.

(f) Scree and talus banks (ST) on the Kigalik River.

www.ingramcontent.com/pod-product-compliance
Lightning Source LLC
Chambersburg PA
CBHW052009280526
45793CB00005B/910